MW00607458

Sailing

IMPRESSIONS
IDEAS
DEEDS

BY

FRANK M. PAPY

Library of Congress Cataloging in
Publication Date 2002
Frank Marin Papy
Sailing Impressions, Ideas, Deeds by Frank Marin Papy
©2001 Library of Congress Number
Printed in The United States of America
Recycled Products Used Wherever Possible

Order from Frank Papy, 87425 Old Highway, #88, Islamorada, Florida 33036
Tel: (305) 852-2326
$12.95 +$2.00 postage and handling.
7% sales tax for Florida residence
ISBN# 0-9619838-6-8

Layout & Design by Tami Music • Editorial Supervision by Carol Music

DEDICATION

This Book is Dedicated To: the late Mister George Gurdjieff
from 1868-1948; my new granddaughter, Morgan Summers
named after a sailboat, a British racing car and a rum; and to
my two goddaughters Marinna and Meghann Williams.

PREFACE

—•—✕◈✕—•—

Living aboard and chartering sailboats for thirty years, I find myself fascinated with everything nautical. I can go to a junk shop or yard sale and spot anything connected with boats or the sea before you can say "Bob is your uncle".

Being the two-year-old that I am I compare this to the finest diploma from MIT. Thank God my wife and daughter love sailing. We find being on the water creates an awareness like no other and I have tried it all. Racing cars, motorcycles, flying and jumping out of a perfectly good airplane. Being on board a sailing vessel, it's a peaceful awareness. But, you must be open to the slightest impressions to take the proper action or you could loose your vessel or the lives of your crew and yourself. That's the rub. It requires the greatest effort, therefore creates the greatest reward. Adventure, passion and madness. We crow like a rooster at the sunrise and howl like a wolf at the moon, listen to music and dance whenever possible.

Many charter captains will keep one another in check. I was told by one of my sailing contemporaries to tone down my nautical exuberance. I must say over the years there are more than several bars and restaurants in the Keys, Bahamas, and Caribbean where I was known to yell upon entering so many times. The bartenders, waitresses and owners would join in in unisonous upon seeing myself, and a charter group after a hard crossing. From some unknown que they would join in "they call me fishmeal", "more rum and fresh whores for my men". We would almost roll on the floor with laughter.

To do something you really love doing and have passion for is truly one of the great pleasures of life.

Job security ~ zero, health insurance ~ zero, retirement ~ zero, like my good friend Captain Dennis says "it's not a job, it's a life style." As I think back on it, I never asked for a raise, I never missed a day being sick and all of this with a bad right knee injured from football, a motorcycle wreck, and a fight. But I found out that having fun is the best painkiller. Sometimes I use a crutch on the boat to help me get around when my knee is bothering me. None of the charters seem to say anything with all this political correctness going around. I used to be called "gimp boat bum", now I am physically challenged, non financially motivated nautical enthusiast.

Some people enrich the world, some people just enrich themselves. In any Cruising Guides of the Keys and Bahamas, I have tried to pass on information that will be helpful to my fellow cruisers. We hope you enjoy this book with a different type of knowledge to enrich the cruising life style.

We are the last of a dying breed.

Author with famous writer, Dick Francs, in Ft. Lauderdale.

ACKNOWLEDGEMENTS

There are some fine people that have helped me out through the years, Cy De Cosse, John Porter, Dan Hardie, Bruce Kessler, Joe Shaffer, Ralph Wilson, Vince Navarro, Colonal D., Pete Andersen, Rose Witte, Eddy Aguero, Bobby Allen, Jim Steel, Dennis and Alice Dugas, Gordon Pennington, Marge Allmand, Shelton Adams, David and Christy Williams, Paul Boatwright, Grondon Bole, Milt Baker, Sam Wampler, Bruce Purdey, Jay Helmken, Mike Brurke, Art Crimmens, Burt Comins, Curtis Tanberg, Tom Collins, Conch Jerry, Garry Corbin, Ted and Louisa Jones, Clark Shimmel, Steve Meramell, Bill Chapple, Malissa Wolin, Bob Gregg, Duke The Dog, Neil Davies, Rob and Dee Dubin, Gary Zaret, Steve Ziskind, Chuck and Corinne Kanter, Jeanne Papy, Willia Youmans, John Smittel, Jimmy Buffet, Russ Teall, Claudia Filippino, The Mystic Mariner, Charly Scarborough, Stuntman, John Ziegler, Captain Winn Jones, Dockmaster Jerry Frances, Fred Wonderlick, and Dick Marble.

Some contributers to Life in St. Kits, West Indies.

TABLE OF CONTENTS

My daughter says she likes the way the book is layed out.
It's like watching MTV! Quick, to the point, and packs a punch!
Jimmy buffett has a song, *Sailing is Like That.*

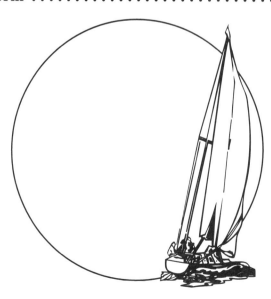

GLOSSARY OF SAILING TERMS

charter sauce *green stuff left in the cooler by charterers*

burner *a charter with white skin and usually red hair*

martyr *a charterer who does all the work others don't want to do*

cutlass *a knife of some kind*

puker *a charter who tends to be sea sick*

sea lawyer *a charterer who knows all the custom laws and the charter contract by heart*

stink pot *power boat, usually diesel*

rag merchant *sail boat captain*

dramamine gulch *the gulf stream*

bugs *spiny lobsters*

flat end or pointy end *words used by charterers to show location of their cabins*

goggle eye *a charterer who watches everything you do*

prom queen *young pretty charter lady who doesn't help because she might break a fingernail*

puffer *charterer who smokes*

splicers *charterers who drink as much as the captain*

profanifobia *what you get when a charterer says they don't like bad language*

flippers *what the charterers call porpoises swimming around the bow*

rags *sails*

iron jib *motor in a sail boat*

porch lights *what charterers call spreader lights*

watching the red TV *compass lights*

bottom dancer *charter captain who runs aground often*

cask *captain's container of rum*

skeger *charterer with a large nose*

galley grinders *teeth or charters who eat alot*

wathcmacallit or thingamajig *what charterers call something when they don't know what it is*

land shark *what charter captains try to avoid*

live stock *term charter captains and brokers use to discuss market*

the jib *proceeds received from selling charterers books, T-shirts, shell necklaces, etc.*

salvage *articles left by charterers*

coconut telegraph *term used to describe the way gossip travels about charter business*

lookout *a signal for other captains not to come aboard; example, a red sock on life line gate*

maiden *A charter boat cook on her first trip*

tumble home *refers to charter captain who had too much rum to walk back to his vessel*

the two block game *any sort of business*

in peril *married charter captain with a bonnie cook aboard*

get spliced *when a person in the marine business gets married*

fish market *good diving reef*

spiked *when a crew member tells on a captain*

porter *boat owner who never leaves the dock*

funnel *crew member who drinks too much*

leech line *another captain's words to get him to lend you money*

scuttle *to get rid of something*

"13" *a code word for a crew to stop what they are doing or saying*

long-legged *sailboat with a deep draft*

zenith *height of a pleasant feeling*

flyer *cooked flying fish seen on W.I. menues – not to be confused with chicken*

check your mizzen *look behind you*

a tender yawl *young southern female charterer*

gaff *money tip from charterer*

a nail *cigarette of some kind*

axis *charterer who asks lots of questions*

scow *charter captain's reference to mother-in-law*

node *hot piece of charcoal that falls from the barbecue grill into the dinghy*

oiler *charterer who refuses to use cream sun tan lotion*

hose *captain with weakness for ladies*

the noon position *captain takes an after lunch nap while charterers are ashore*

travil *things you take to the beach for a cook-out*

two blocks *to draw up too far*

pump room *what charters call the head*

ready about *back to back charters*

rhumb line *what a north captain says to talk you out of some free drinks*

sea mules *term for some delivery captains*

dog watch *a boat with very unattractive passengers*

pump the bilge *go to the head*

shanty'ems *W.I. people who come in your boat to sing and play for money*

sheet wench *lady with lots of boy friends*

shell shocked *charterers who go shelling and come upon nude sunbathers*

deck ape *crew used for muscle power only*

shoal water *term for strong rum*

keel *captain or crew's backbone*

signal yard *charter captain's right arm*

trimaran *sailboat with training wheels*

stabilizer *code for having owner or manager aboard*

apogee *doing a charter to bury someone at sea*

IN THE BEGINNING

Well, when my aunt's new boyfriend gave me the boat, I put a sail on it and named her the "Sea Raven." In the meantime, I fell in love with a girl named Carmen Cherry. That's a funny name isn't it? Having a passion for sailing, fixing up the boat, and thinking about her gave me extra energy. Her family had a summer place in Bluffton, S.C. that was about twenty miles away by water. I knew she went over there every weekend. I had seen her in school but I was a little shy, so I thought I would sail over there, tie up to her dock, and then invite her to go sailing. They would all be down on the dock and see me sail up and be very impressed, and I could take her sailing and she would fall madly in love with me. I got my boat all ready, packed up a lunch, put a blanket in there, and a flashlight. I had all the charts, and I had my little motor gassed up. So I set out on Saturday morning at dawn. Well, with the tide, the wind, and my sailing skills, my little motor and I didn't make it there until dawn the next morning. I anchored for a while, rested, and finally saw their dock. I managed to tie up Sunday morning around six. I was so tired I just laid down in the boat. About an hour later I heard somebody clearing his throat. I looked up and I saw Carmen's father.

"What are you doing there, son?"

I said, "Well, I sailed around from Fox Island."

He said, "What did you do that for?"

"Well, I had this idea."

"What kind of ideas you got?"

"I really like sailing, and I met your daughter at school, and I thought I would sail around here and see if she wanted to go sailing."

"When did you leave over there at Fox Island?"

"Saturday morning at 6:00."

He said, "Wow, that took a while to get here."

So, I started to tell him the story. He took a look at the boat, went up to his house and came back with a cup of coffee for me. He broke the news to me that Carmen was going with an older guy, Mike Bonner, who was the Olympic challenger for javelin throwing. But, he said that I was welcome to stay at the dock and come up for lunch. Then Carmen came down and looked at the boat and I had a nice long talk with her. I sailed back to Fox Island. What an experience that was! Now that I think back on it, it was very interesting that my mother trusted me totally. That I was gone all night and didn't call was something that was accepted.

Carmen's father had told me, "Next time you like a girl, why don't you call her up and see if she wants to go sailing rather than sail all the way over to her place?"

I said, "Thanks, that sure is some good advice, I appreciate that." But then, later, at school, Carmen put in some good words for me with some other girls, and things really worked out for sailing, having fun, and hanging out at the yacht club.

I went to a little two year junior college and taught some more sailing, and then went off to the national guard to boot camp. My family was in the shipping business. When I came back I started off as a time keeper and worked my way up to stevedore and foreman. They had offices in Ft. Lauderdale, Mobile, and New Orleans. I went down to Ft. Lauderdale and was working part time. John Porter came down on a converted twelve meter yawl and docked it at Bahia Mar, one of the nicest marinas in Ft. Lauderdale. Phil Flashman was the Captain and wanted to do some charters on her to make some extra money for the owner to pay for dockage and insurance. He said he was going to leave her down there all winter.

John and I met some girls and some other people at one of the yacht clubs there and we took them out sailing. They sent a few people over. Everyone just wanted to go sailing for free. John and I had met a couple of flight attendants and they said they would pay to go over to Freeport. They wanted to sail over to the Bahamas to buy scotch and gin and things like that because it was so much cheaper than it was in the States. We did one sail over there, and I think they bought two cases of gin. Beaffeters gin was about twelve dollars a case and scotch was the same. When we came back in, we cleared customs and the customs man charged us about twenty-five cents a bottle duty.

That customs charge was so small we got the idea to put notices up on the bulletin boards at the different airlines in Ft. Lauderdale, Miami, and Palm Beach that said you could come down and charter a twelve meter and sail on over to the Bahamas for booze. You could leave on Friday night at five in the evening and be back by five Monday morning. I think we charged thirty dollars a head, and said you could buy enough liquor to pay for the trip. When we started doing that, we were pretty much booked up. We would take three couples, sometimes six girls or six guys, and sail over to Grand Bahama and anchor off west end.

Sometimes we would go into the Jack Tar Hotel. This boat had a pretty deep draft. They would come back aboard after buying cloth, Scottish wool, tweed by the yard, and liquor. We got to know the customs men. We would come in on Monday morning and clear customs, everyone would go off to work, and we'd have the rest of the week off. I would pick up a few day sails, and then I started getting time for my captain's license. John and I were just having a ball. I met a guy named Leo, who had a boat named the "Davinta." He and his wife were stunt people in the circus in Canada (they dove off a high tower into a little tank) and we sailed over to the Bahamas and Nassau. This is how I got to know Bimini and the Berry Islands. It was beautiful.

When we would put the boat at anchor, I would take the dinghy to row around and explore. I met the guy, Harry Kline, who was doing the Bahama Guide at the time and learned some neat spots to go to, and how nice the people were.

There were a lot of lobsters and fish. I learned how to dive, snorkel, spear fish, and get conch. You could feed yourself, just ride the wind and get your food from the sea. It was terrific. We would come back to Ft. Lauderdale, meet some of the owners on some of the other boats, and take them out on their boats as a guide. That's how I got into the charter boat business. Then I went down to New Orleans and sailed with my cousin, Cookie Keenan out of the Southern Yacht Club, on the "Swiftshore." It was a really nice boat that belonged to Burt Keenan, his brother, who later sailed "Louisiana Crude" to victory in the Southern Ocean Racing Circuit. We sailed the New Orleans to Mobile race, a Gulf port race. We sailed through the rigger leaves. Everybody had to juggle their time, because they had to raise the bridge. New Orleans was really terrific with all the food, sailing, and the nice people. I loved it over there, and stayed with my cousin Frank Strachan. They lived in Jefferson Davis's White House. I worked there on the waterfront. They transferred me to Mobile. After having too much rum, I drove a pickup truck through the doors of Mary's Irish Channel Bar. I stayed out of there for a while. I went back to Miami where I joined the Miami Business Man's Boating Association. They had a Cat Ketch, an old Catamaran, and a 30 foot sloop that you could use anytime you wanted to. When I wasn't loading and unloading ships, I was over there sailing and taking other people out sailing. I learned the waters of Biscayne Bay, which were beautiful. They were unbelievable. Then, I made several trips over to the Bahamas, and down into the Keys. I learned the waters and met a lot of interesting people. We caught a lot of fish. I found a 24 foot wooden sloop a "Munn. design" She drew four feet and had a little Kermath gasoline engine. I bought her for two thousand dollars and kept her on the Miami River at Hardies Marina. What a trip that was going up and down the Miami River and going out into Biscayne Bay. So, every minute that I wasn't working, I was out sailing. Mr. Hardie, his uncle, and the people at Hardie's Marina were fascinated by the passion that I had for boating and sailing.

They got me work and gave me a lot of good advice. One time, I told them about a delivery I was doing. I had to take a 60-ft. Ketch to New York, and Mr. Hardie said, "Just remember take it one day at a time. If you think about the whole thing it will overwhelm you. Just say, 'Today if I get to Palm Beach it will be a miracle.' And that's what I did. It worked out perfectly. I had a lot of trouble along the way but there were some terrific times. I started doing more delivery work.

I always wondered, "who am I"? Now I know, I'm a sailor. When you really have a passion for something like sailing, you really love it. Then, when you're not doing it, you're reading about it, thinking about it, and watching it on t.v. every minute.

The three rules of sailing are, never be in hurry, don't spit into the wind, and don't sail where the trees grow.

When I wrote the book Cruising Guide to the Florida Keys, people would say, "Wow, that really helped me out a lot. I was in a tight spot down there and read your book and it got me out of trouble."

John Porter and I used to go down and catch shiners off the dock with a dip net, and then catch trout. The yacht club had an open air house by the pool, a mini club house for the young people. John and I would catch enough fish to have a fish fry for about twenty-five of those young people. They would supply the beer, cokes, paper plates, knives, and forks, and we would fry up all those fish and have a ball. I had a friend who had a Sunfish sailboat. I would trailer it down to the back river of Savannah Beach, put it into the water, and sail it around to the ocean side of the island.

We would go to a place called the Novelty Bar, have a couple of beers, and sail it back around. The ocean here has really strange currents.

Back in those days you didn't worry about stuff as much. It was a more relaxed era in the late fifties and early sixties. There wasn't a crime problem and gasoline was around twenty-eight cents a gallon. A rum and coke was twenty-five cents. No one worried about insurance and life seemed easy. It was a different time, so my friend Jazz Marino said.

As in life, so with big boat deliveries, you can't get jobs without experience, and you can't get experience without jobs. But I found a way to beat it. There were about five yacht brokers in Ft. Lauderdale. Every morning I would get up, ride my bike or take the car up to the brokers office, meet the secretaries, and have a cup of coffee. I would sit around the office, maybe run an errand for them or something. I would then go to the next brokers office, ask them if they had any business, wait around the waiting room and read a few magazines. Often they would need something done, and I would help them do it.

I just kept doing that and remained persistent. Finally, they got a call for something they didn't want to do, sort of that

Captain Ron thing. They said there was an English Cutter down in Jamaica. She was up in the yard and they wanted to take it up to Ft. Lauderdale, and sell it or something. They called around and couldn't find any captains that wanted to go down to Jamaica to take this Old Wooden English Cutter that had a tiller. Can you imagine a fifty-five foot boat with a tiller on it? Anyway, they said, "Where is that kid that hangs around the office all the time? Call him in here. " OK, I tell you what we are going to pay you fifty dollars a day and fly you down to Jamaica. See if you can round up a crew down there. We will pay their airfare back, and you all can bring this boat back up to Ft. Lauderdale. You can go in the room there and get some charts for it". So I flew down to Jamaica, and the boat was in the yard. She was pretty nautical down below but she had been sitting up for about a year and a half. We put her in the water, and she swelled up pretty good. I got the engine running and I met a Jamaican kid who said he would go along, and then a religious fanatic who came around the boat yard. He was about twenty years old, and was preaching trying to get everyone to become religious. He needed a ride back to the states, so he said he would come along. I figured we would use him for manpower.

Then I met Theresa. She and I became real good friends. She was on another boat down there, but said she would come along to help me sail the cutter back up to the states. This was in September.

I figured hurricane season must be over but they didn't have all the satellite stuff in those days. You mostly got the information from ships and planes. So, we left out of Jamaica and started heading up towards the states. We got into a tropical depression. The winds were about fifty-sixty knots for three days. And it was unbelievable. She would run at five knots under bare poles, with nothing up.

I kept the old Gardner Diesel Engine running and that made her fairly stable. I couldn't take a sun sight with my Sextant so I was pretty much navigating by the seat of my pants, you might say, on time and distance, holding a compass course. The noise in three days of it blowing like that was just unbelievable. It will drive you nuts. Tom, my religious free ride to Ft. Lauderdale, had a nervous breakdown, what I called the catatonic eclipse. He went down below, got around the base of the mast, went into the fetal position, and started speaking an unknown tongue. Theresa broke her finger in one of the blocks as she was handling the tiller. But Terry, the Jamaican kid, could steer the best.

He was in a trance and didn't seem to care one way or the other. It was unbelievable keeping that boat upright. She leaked badly through the decks and it was tough keeping the pumps going.

We were moving along with the tropical depression as it shifted we just stayed in it. I had been up for seventy-two hours. Something happened to my eyes, they would just stick open or closed and wouldn't operate properly. The boat had cotton caulking in it and the chain plates were pulling so hard on the hull that it started spreading the planking. The caulking was coming out, and she started leaking badly. If I could keep the batteries charged with the old diesel and keep the engine running, I knew I could keep the water down. If she got too bad, the whole boat would fill up.

The "Life Boat" was an old, rotten, heavy jolly boat, unfit for these seas. so, I knew we'd have to stick with our ship. We had an old AM radio, and I just couldn't get anything on that but static. The caulking got so bad I knew the water was going to come up over the engine. I had pretty much given up. I put my head down on the table and thought I had had a good life. I was only 23. Then, I thought of the tool box. In the bottom of that box was some chicken wire that had a half inch mesh. I started thinking that the diesel uses sea water to cool the engine. So, if I closed the sea cock to the raw water supply to the diesel engine, I could put that chicken wire around the hose, stick it down in the bilge, and pump that water out of the boat to cool the engine-through the exhaust system. It was like a light bulb that went off in my head as in the comic books.

I had been up eighty hours now, Theresa had a broken finger, and I had the Jamaican kid to steer but that was it. It took me two hours to disconnect that hose, close the sea cock, and put the chicken wire over the end of the hose because 40 years accumulation of trash had floated up with the rising water.

There was saw dust, and God knows what else was clogging up that bilge pump. I kept the engine running and finally the wind died down. I figured out where Great Anaugra was and we sailed her there.

Some of the locals helped me careen the boat and an old guy helped me put some of the caulking back in and straighten things up. I took the money that I had, forty-five dollars, and flew my religious man, Tom, home. A local preacher took him out of the boat, put him to bed in his house for two days, and then got him on the plane to Ft. Lauderdale. I never did hear any more from that kid. God bless him.

We picked up another American girl in Great Anaugra who wanted a ride as far as Nassau. The weather was good from then on and we got the boat straightened out. It was a really interesting experience ~ I didn't think I was going to die ~ I knew I was going to die. I was just wondering if drowning was going to be bad. When I got to Great Anaugra, the people there said, "You've been through this storm, that's hard to believe… I think that boat was on the deck of a ship and got washed overboard or something." We finally got the boat up to Ft. Lauderdale, walked up the dock and into the brokers office. When I told them I had tied the boat to their dock, they laughed and shook their heads and said under their breath, "That boat was supposed to sink on the way up here."

After that I looked at life a whole different way. When somebody told me your cleaning isn't ready yet, it didn't make a difference. I'd think about being out on that boat and almost dying. When I get into a tight spot, I look back on that experience and think, whatever doesn't kill you may make you stronger, somehow or other, in the struggle of life.

Something I've noticed chartering is that people who eat a lot of seafood don't get sea sick. That's the only thing I can think of to explain this. And if you do get sea sick, stay on deck and keep looking at the horizon so that your mind knows what's going on. Perhaps it's something in your inner ear that makes you dizzy. In all my years of chartering, I guess I have seen more people throw up than the average doctor. They have thrown up in the compass, in the rubber boots, and in the sink going down below. One fellow threw up and lost his glasses and false teeth overboard. We were in Nassau and he wanted to go to the casino. So we went to a Nassau dentist who had a lot of teeth in a shoe box. That dentist used a grinder motor to trim the teeth down and make him a set. We went to the Goodwill store and they had about twenty eye glasses, so he tried on a couple using the newspaper as an eye chart and picked out a pair. The whole thing cost about $20. We were set to go the casino. We were big time.

SPINY URCHINS AND
ISLAND MEDICAL CARE

I was the charter skipper aboard the *Anetria,* a converted 12 Meter, down in Jamaica. Our last charter had carried us west along the coast to Port Royal. We tied up at the Prince George Marina, waiting for instructions for our next trip. My cook/mate was a swell Canadian named Annie. A true cordon bleu chef, very energetic, and she had been a stunt double for Elke Summers. In this job she met my favorite actor and writer, the late Sterling Hayden on the movie set and some wild stories to tell about parties and escapades. Normally, during this period on board, I would be resting, but with Annie buzzing with energy all the time, we had to go diving. We took the dinghy over to an old ruins to see if we could spear some dinner. I found a cave about 10 feet deep with seven nice big lobsters hiding out in the end. My first trip down I got one with my Hawaiian sling. On my second dive, to show off with Miss Annie watching, I bagged two bugs and was doing my usual "panic method of diving."

A lady on one of my charters asked me one time, "Captain, how do you free dive?" I told her I never really thought about it, but that I guess I panic dive. "What's that?" says she.

"Oh, I guess I go down until I don't have any more breath left, and say, 'Holy Moley, I better head for the surface.'"

That's the spot that I was in this time with those two bugs on my spear in that cave. With not enough air in my lungs left to turn around, I decided I'd better back out. That's when it happened. There were spiny urchins growing down in the top of that cave and I jammed about six spines into my left heel.

Being "Mister Macho", I didn't give it much thought until about an hour later when the heel started to throb.

If you're not acquainted with spiny urchins, they have this group of ice picks sticking out from the body about six inches. They grow in a bunch of about 20 or 30. They are hollow, made out of something like thin glass with poisoned barbs which pierce your skin, and you can't pull them out. When you try to grab them with tweezers it just crushes them.

After about 2 days I was ready for anything that would stop the pain. The lady at the marina said the hotel doctor was away for a week, just my luck. Her only suggestion was to go to the public clinic in Kingston, a cab ride away. I hobbled along quite well with a cane and Annie's shoulder to lean on with a lot of gauze wrapped around my heel, a warning for passers-by.

The waiting room was pretty crowded with Jamaicans, one of whom gave up a chair and a stool to prop my foot on. Annie slipped off to find the nurse. About 20 minutes had gone by when the doctor and his assistant came out into the waiting room. He was about 6'5", and with his long white coat he looked like a giant. He asked quite politely if I was the yank with the urchins in my heel. I said yes, and right there in the waiting room he began to unwrap the gauze from around my foot. The nurse and Annie moved around to the back of my chair.

In a flash the white coated doctor pulled a large chrome plated ball peen hammer from under his clipboard and gave my heel about three hard whacks. The pain was like a flash bulb going off in my face. I tried to jump up and give him a hard right cross on the jaw, but Annie and the nurse grabbed me. I sat back down in a daze, looked around the waiting room, and no one was even giving us a second glance. It must be a normal event judging from their reactions. Anyway, I let out a couple of sailor's choice cuss words, and asked what the hell he thought he was doing. The doctor replied in his slow Jamaican drawl, "I crushed them up and I will give you some pills to help them dissolve into your system, you will be as good as new, and will be sailing in a couple of days, Captain."

I said as politely as I could, "Your bedside manner leaves something to be desired."

"Okay", he replied, "I take you into the examining room, show you the hammer, and tell you what I'm going to do. What would be your reaction?"

"I would have walked out."

He said, "Well, you see, we eliminated all of that. It's going to cost you $3.00 and here are your pills. I am glad I had the nurse and your mate stand behind you, you are pretty fast with that right cross. I used to box a bit in college myself you know."

Well, sure enough, my heel got well in a couple of days. The doctor and his wife stopped by for drinks to see how I was doing. His wife asked me what I thought of the clinic's medical treatment.

"I am cured, and it only cost $3.00", I said, "and the doctor came by the boat to see how I was. That's not bad by any standards."

She seemed quite pleased. A good thing I was well, as the next day we picked up our charters from Ocho Rios and the first thing out of their mouths was, "We want to do a lot of lobster diving." Annie gave me a cautious look, and I thought to myself, *what a beautiful world.*

Sea Urchins

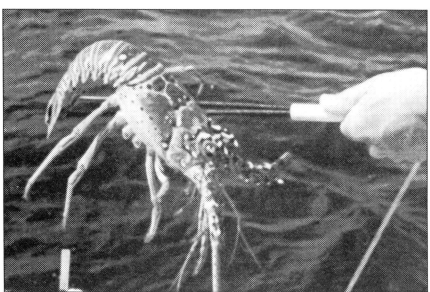

UNDERWATER REVENGE

—◆— ⪤◆⪥ —◆—

I sneaked away from my scout charter after we had docked in Marathon Key, slipped upstairs for a quick cool one from my favorite lady bar tender, Cindy, and got a scowl and a rather subdued greeting. "You've got to cut it out," Cindy said, "I can't keep a straight face anymore, hearing about your pranks."

It seems a boat from New Jersey had been tied up in Marathon for several days and Cindy had become friends with the crew. On about their third afternoon at the bar, she asked if they had gotten a chance to snorkel out on the reef yet. They related a wild story about a guy catching and wrestling a large barracuda underwater, beating its head onto a ladder and throwing it onto a sailboat. Cindy, being a good sport and not wanting to punch any holes in their high adventure story asked, "Do you remember the name of this sailboat?" They replied, "The *Janake*, or *Jakey*, or something like that." She remembered I was on the *Jenicka*, put two and two together, and asked for more details.

Well, the real story is, earlier in the week, a boat from New Jersey had given me a big wake, passing a bit too close. I didn't yell at them, not wanting to set a bad example for my young crew. Anyway, about 2 days later, I found myself moored on the reef right next to them. My crew had gone snorkeling and we had a couple of big barracudas, we'd caught earlier, lying on the back deck. I was saving them for a friend who uses them as chum. When I decided to go in myself, I noticed the Jersey boat crew was also getting ready to go snorkeling. As I slipped down into the water over the stern ladder, I pulled the biggest barracuda in with me. It wasn't quite stiff yet, and I figured I'd give the Jersey group a little scare. They were snorkeling right by my stern, so, I braced my flipper on the ladder and swung behind the big barn door rudder to hide. When they got near, I shot the barracuda out in front of them, you could hear them through their snorkels, "oooh, aaah!" It was working great until the cuda started to sink. I appeared out of nowhere, grabbed the fish by the gills and the tail, and began a fake wrestling match, making the fish look as alive as possible, as I fought the silver demon. As I was getting tired, I wrestled closer to the stainless steel swimming ladder and banged the fish's head into the ladder several times, then placed one flipper on the ladder and flung the fish up on the back deck, yelling expletives. Then I moved quickly around to the bow, looking for another fish to wrestle.

As the sea gods would have it, the hatch was open, and the barracuda slid down into the aft cabin, giving me about a half hour of cleaning fish slime off the rug, but the prank was worth every minute of it.

HENDRICKS ISLE

I sailed into Ft. Lauderdale ten years ago with my wife and daughter on the *Lamara II,* our forty-five-foot Mason ketch. Looking for secure dock space we stumbled across Hendricks Isle. We found a nice spot behind an eight unit apartment building with four live-aboards in the back. We met Pierre and Mitzi, the owners, and had worked out a deal for a slip until they saw my four-year-old daughter.

Sorry, no kids, no pets."

My daughter said, "Daddy, what's wrong?

I said, "Don't know ~ go ask the man." She talked to him for about five minutes. To this day, I don't know what she said, but we got the slip.

Now for those readers who think living aboard is a rough life ashore, when we were not out sailing, we had showers, washer, dryer, swimming pool, heated Jacuzzi, cable TV, patio with a gas BBQ grill, ping-pong table, an aviary with seventeen exotic birds and one hundred and seventy-five rose bushes on the property to keep things smelling sweet. Pierre maintained excellent security, left over from his days in the military. Hendricks Isle, right off Las Olas Boulevard, which is the heart of Fort Lauderdale, is convenient to everything: stores, doctors, dentists, banks, and a fantastic public library and a brand new art museum.

For the first five years we were there my wife didn't drive so she used a bicycle and our dinghy for means of transportation through the elaborate and little-known canal systems of Fort Lauderdale.

Later, when she was driving the car (she still preferred the dinghy) twelve minutes to school, fifteen minutes to downtown. She even took my daughter to dancing lessons at the Fort Lauderdale Yacht Club in the dinghy, a twenty-minute ride, especially during the tourist season when the traffic is very heavy on the ' highways and byways.

My favorite part of living aboard was getting up on a Sunday morning, having a leisurely breakfast in the cockpit, reading the newspaper and then taking a ride up the river with my family. My wife brought her harmonica and an umbrella, and my daughter grabbed her cabbage patch doll and we set off for a pleasant cruise, either stopping at Shirtail Charlie's or the Ancient Marines for lunch or stopping at one of the parks along the river for a picnic. Our favorite was Colee Hammock Park with it's beautiful giant old oak trees, truly paradise on the water.

With the difficulty of children on the island we thought it would be a problem for our daughter, but it was great. There are quite a few kids who live in the apartments and houses, and many other children on the cruising boats that come through. To me, children who grow up on sailboats are very special. They seem different than the children from the land. I guess it's because space is so limited on a boat, they can't have too much stuff to get spoiled. In my opinion, they appreciate nature more. I suppose, it's being closer to it on the water. We feed the seagulls and an occasional manatee that wanders through.

My daughter, who is twelve now, has about a dozen pen pals all over the world who are kids of cruising parents. Reading these letters is an education in itself, all the different far away lands, customs and behaviors.

Most of the cruising sailors seem to have a strange fascination for Fort Lauderdale, and end up stopping back through on their way to and from the Caribbean.

As a yacht captain and writer I get many opinions of this fantastic city, both positive and negative. The main complaint from these world cruisers is the fact that there are no good anchorages or reasonable prices for the dockage. There is one anchorage by the Las Olas bridge, which is open water, free most anywhere else to anchor. These sailors are quite shocked after anchoring and then finding out when a policeman comes by and wants $12 a day from a city who benefits from their visitation, both culturally and monetarily, not to mention the aesthetics of a beautiful sleek sailing vessel anchored in the harbor with a bevy of beauties aboard.

So in turn, they travel up the New River, tie up to the seawall at the city docks which are right on the street and find out it costs $600 a month for a 50-footer. Back home that would be a mortgage payment on a small house. They complain and leave in disgust for places up the coast and down to the Keys for municipalities who place more value on the visitation of a cruising sailor.

In my 8-year stay at Hendricks Isle, the owner of the docks where we moored was under constant pressure for pollution, fire hazard, and a ten-foot easement between the buildings from the City Administration who call themselves the "Yachting Capital of the World." I hope someday they open their eyes and help instead of hinder sailors and powerboaters who are passing through and the ones who make their homes here. I think they see boating people as two classes: boat bums, who they want to run out with their high prices, or the super-rich who they want and don't care how much they pay for dockage. In there, I am sure, is a happy middle class somewhere.

God Bless the city fathers who see their way clear to give an advantage to those who bring benefits to the community and I hope this humble literary endeavor will help shed some light on the sunny waterways of Fort Lauderdale.

Ellie Papy on board Lamara.

Our home for 10 years, 45 foot Mason.

Office in forepeak.

MY MOST
CHALLENGING CHARTER

I was catching up with maintenance on my boat, so it was temporarily out of commission. That's when I received a call from Colonel Joe, who said he'd caught some kind of terrible flu bug and asked if I could help him out by taking the charter he had lined up.

"There are 24 ultra-conservative religious young people coming in from Ohio", he told me, "and the boat's a 65 foot plywood and fiberglass ketch. The owner is not going along, it will be your show."

"What's the rub?" I said. "There must be something else."

"They don't eat what you eat." says he. "All they eat is vegetables. They even bring their own pans." I asked him when all of this was to take place. Joe said he was supposed to meet the owner of the charter vessel at 10:00 on the dock, and it was already 10:30. So I grabbed my gear, turned on the answering machine, and snagged a ride down to the marina.

Jack, the owner, said he was in a big hurry, handed me a portable VHF radio, with the comment that there were problems with the ship's VHF radio, and he turned around and started to leave.

"Hey," says I, "How about showing me around a little bit, eh?" He said, "It's all here, no problem."

Looking around below, it appeared that I was the only one who was going to have a cabin. The rest of the boat was wide open. Looking forward from the companionway ladder, there was a long table with benches on either side, forward of that was the head. It consisted of a rack to hold 2 one gallon water jugs. There was a dowel sticking out of the bulkhead with two rolls of bathroom stationary and a large black bucket strong enough to sit on. The door was a curtain made out of blue canvas. Forward of the head were 12 bunks, port and starboard, for a total of 24. The lowers were single and the uppers were doubles, compact to say the least. It was like pictures I've seen of slave ships. I threw my sea bag and gear in the little aft cabin, took a tour of the deck, and put on my mask and fins to take a look at the hull.

When I surfaced, staring over the rail were 24 inquisitive young faces. I told them I was a part-time troll who lived under the boat and had taken the job to be their captain. I didn't think they got the humor, so I went on deck and got them to start loading their gear aboard.

A captain from a big power boat a few slips over, came over to find out where I was going to fit all these people. I didn't know his name, although I had seen him around. He was perusing the food being loaded aboard ~ all beans, fruit, and vegetables. I told him it was a two week charter to Nassau. He just shook his head and turned and walked toward his big white "Howard Johnson" afloat.

A little while later his cook showed up with a box with four large Genoa salamis, two bottles of Vat 19 rum, a pillow, pillowcase, and two bed sheets. The cook told me her Captain said to only drink one bottle a week, no more, and bring back 2 replacements from Nassau (the only place I know, outside of Trinidad, where one can get Vat 19).

We had a nice crossing of the Gulf Stream, with a stiff southerly wind of about 15 knots and a three-quarter moon, so I could keep an eye on the shipping traffic. I'd never before had a crew of 24 so I assigned them duties, a "steering crew", an "up-the-sail crew", and a "down-the-sail crew." I figured I would learn their names later on, but it was really hard, because they referred to themselves as "sister" this and "brother" that. At first they called me "Brother Captain", but I got them to change it to "Brother Frank."

There was a pretty good ground swell running, and about half of them got seasick crossing the "Dramamine Gulch." They would run for the lee rail to flash, and as it was nighttime I asked their leader, whom I called Brother Head Preacher, to assign barf buddies ~ another crew member to watch over his partner to keep him from falling over the rail when heaving. It's the safest thing to do. Unfortunately, it usually makes the barf buddy sick, too, but that's better than having to look for somebody overboard at night.

There was a beautiful sunrise, and we got into Bimini at 07:30. There weren't too many good appetites after the night at sea, but I borrowed a couple of eggs from the boat next door and had a nice breakfast.

When we had cleared customs, the group made a tour of the island's churches. As a special present for me, they brought back imitation hamburgers made out of soybean meal. I tried them, but... I went for the salami, washed down with Vat 19. They thought me most peculiar. In fact, they were really very nice, well-meaning folks, just not the type I usually run with.

Jerry, the dockmaster came on board, to play the guitar and sing for us. They were thrilled to hear the island music and were very good singers themselves.

The next day we headed for the Berry Islands, 86 miles across the great Bahama banks. It was a hot day with very little breeze. We were motoring along at about 8 knots, and to break the monotony, I let out a couple of fishing lines off the stern.

Our first fish was a barracuda of about 25 pounds. I gaffed him and cracked him in the head with a winch handle. Brother

Head Preacher was very displeased. He said I should have let him go without hurting him. The next one we caught was even bigger than the first. I got it on deck and told Brother Head Preacher he could let him go if he wanted to, but just then the barracuda took a big swipe at him with those big teeth, and ~ *blap* ~ Brother Head Preacher hit it in the head with the winch handle. "That barracuda is the devil in disguise", he said. We caught one more mackerel before we anchored in a nice little cove in Chub Cay in time for a snorkeling trip to the nearby Mama Rhoda Rock.

This was the first time any of the kids ever had their heads under the water. After they got their masks and snorkles adjusted, I led expeditions over to the reef, where they had their first glimpse of the beautiful colored fish, coral, and sea fans. I could feel their excitement. It was like being transported to another world.

All made it back to the boat without incident; I had Brother Head Preacher do a head count to make sure. Then came a million questions. What kind of fish was that? What was this, etc, etc? So, I picked six hearty rowers and we launched the dinghy and headed for a large fancy power boat with diving tanks on the stern. There were several couples on the aft deck having cocktails. I quieted their nervous looks by saying this was a religious group, not pirates. I asked if I could please speak to the captain, and when he came I explained my predicament and asked to borrow some identification books on fish and coral. He was very accommodating and gave me three excellent books. My young passengers were up most of the night looking up at the stars and talking about what they had seen under the sea. After that, I could not keep them out of the water.

On the last day a big squall came through the anchorage

around 1500. A French couple on a boat anchored next to us came topside, naked, to take a shower in the rain. This freaked out Brother Head Preacher and he ordered me to pull up the anchors and head for Nassau. This was counter productive, as all the kids had to be on deck to pull up those two rusty old 75-pound anchors. They had a grand bird's eye view of the uninhibited couple taking their shower *au natural.*

We had a good run home to Miami and caught about a 26 pound wahoo in the Gulf Stream. On the way, the alternator belt broke and I made one out of a piece of 3/8" nylon line with a long splice in it. The fram fuel filter clogged up and we made one out of three white cotton socks.

As it turned out, my crew was great, once we got used to each other's ways. The boat was another story. I guess you could call that trip the "achievable nightmare."

Sailing dingy on the front porch.

YOURS OR SOMEBODY ELSE'S?

In 1977 I had my own charter boat, a ketch-rigged Morgan Out Island 41. Life was sweet. My wife and I lived aboard an Islander 33, and we were squeaking by, chartering 12 weeks per year and picking up some delivery work on the side. That's when I got a call from one of the local brokers. He was working on a deal to sell an Irwin 52, and his client wanted to interview six skippers to pick one to be his regular captain. I said I wasn't interested because I had my own charter boat. Besides, I wasn't interested in a regular job.

Well, about cocktail hour, the broker calls again. "Hey Paps, I got five captains to come in tomorrow, how about if I give you a full day's pay to come in and get interviewed for the job?"

I says, "Suppose I get the job?"

He says, "Who, out of all the captains you know, can be bad enough to not get the job.?"

So, the next day, I found myself surrounded by five other captains waiting for the call to go into the broker's office and tell their story of how they would run this new Irwin 52. With the broker looking like an expectant father, waiting for the birth of his big commission, we were two down, and I was called next.

I was dressed in my usual scruffy boat shoes, stained khaki shorts, with a knife stuck in my belt, and dark glasses to enhance my assumed look of unconcern, I strutted into the office, flopped down in the overstuffed leather chair and threw one leg up over an arm. I looked up and said, "Hey, Commodore."

Commodore looked me over, then asked, "What is your specialty?" He kinda caught me off guard, so I asked him what he meant. "Well", the Commodore continued, "the first captain said his specialty was making the boat go fast. The second captain said his specialty was knowing all of the good diving spots. So, what's yours.

I piped up as cocky as I could and said my specialty was having a good time.

He caught me off guard again, because he said, "Well, I guess you're hired."

"Whoa", I said, "I don't really want a regular job, I have my own charter boat and…"

Undaunted, the Commodore said he guessed he really didn't need a full-time captain. He wanted to know about my charter business, then said we should give it a try. "You and I will fly to St. Petersburg, and you can fix the boat up any way you like."

Well, that was the clincher, so we left the office and the Commodore told the broker to let the other captains go, he'd found his man. The broker was in shock. I met the Commodore's family, and we went to St. Pete and delivered the boat to Miami.

We had a ball fixing up the boat. I used words I'd only seen in the magazines: roller furling, electric winches ~ we even had roller furling on the mizzen. It was great.

The first trip was like a charter, then I began to see the difference. Every time I docked the boat, it had to be perfect, as every eye seems to be judging your every move. Another difficulty is that the owner meets other owners and captains who are constantly giving suggestions: "We do it this way", and, "My captain does it that way." This can create awkward situations when you have the boat set up to do things a certain way. Or, you recommend not going out because of a bad weather forecast, but the other captain goes out and the weather turns fair in the afternoon, so your owner is disappointed because he didn't get to go sailing.

On the up side, the pay is fantastic, and the Commodore worked out his sailing schedule around my charters. However, when you are on your own boat, you are accepted automatically as "The Captain."

One time, I arrived aboard the Commodore's boat after the guests were all aboard. One of the ladies said, "Well, he looks like a captain with his beard, shorts, boat shoes, and a big watch." "Is that a Rolex?' she asked. "No, it's an imitation", I told her. "Well, don't most good yacht captains have a Rolex?" "Yes, Ma'am", I replied, and went about my business.

We sailed through a fairly narrow channel, and there was another large sailboat not far off. I looked at it through a pair of binoculars. The lady asked me what I was looking at, and I told her that I was looking at the big sailboat over there.

"Well", she said, "It's close enough, you can see that without looking through binoculars."

"Yes, Ma'am", I said with my most polite southern-boy charm, "I'm checking to see if the captain over there is wearing a Rolex."

Later, the Commodore said he had heard the conversation and almost bit through his lip to keep from laughing.

Sometimes, the Commodore would invite my wife and

daughter to come along to Nassau for the weekend so I wouldn't be so cranky. A charter captain would never be able to do that. That covers some of the difference between being a captain for a private owner and charter jobs. All in all, I like the charters better. I think it is because of their enthusiasm and excitement over sailing and being out in the ocean air. Also, with a charter I am always being surprised by the different reactions of different people. I guess a true sailor is always fascinated by the unknown.

Taken by Mary Ann Gibson, 1974, Bahamas.

BOAT SHOW SHENANIGANS

After the boat show we had a little party at our station. In fine attendance were the folks from the GPS booth and, in sharp contrast, the representatives from the booth which sold sextants, where I had gotten into trouble earlier in the show. Being a firm believer that on a long ocean voyage one should have a sextant and a chronometer, and the proper tables to back up any electrical navigation device, usually keeps me in good stead with them. However, when they weren't looking, I took some black electrical tape and taped my very small GPS to the handle of their finest sextant, which fit quite well, and placed it back in the box. Chuck, an old sea dog friend, then went over and picked it up and said in amazement, "What a great idea, a sextant with a GPS in the handle, the best of both worlds." Several other patrons in the booth began to question them about this innovation, "What's the price, etc." As they all looked at one another in amazement and surprise, I figured Chuck and I had gotten enough mileage out of our joke, so I stepped over before anger set in, and said, "Your sextant is like your credit card, never leave home without it! The electrical devices are nice, but it's always good to have a back up." That broke the tension and we got a good round of laughter, my favorite sound other than the wave under the bowsprit at seven knots. Now, how can I think of a way to tape a paper chart to one of these new computer screen charts? Tune in next time for more boat show mania.

Where do I get all these adventurous ideas asked my editor. "Why, from you," says I, "the man who knows how to make a square barge out of a round tank."

I had the pleasure of writing a regular column for Capt. Ted Jones and his charming wife "Miss Louisa." What fun we had delivering sail boats and living aboard at the Annapolis Show anchored out. Party, party, party.

"Chi Chi S" S.O.R.C. Phil Handleman.

GOOD SAILING IN THE FUTURE

What have we got to show, so far, for this year? Tristan Jones, God bless him, has died in Thailand. He was a fantastic writer and we will miss his good works. We lost the America's Cup to New Zealand and watched the Australian boat break in half and sink in 3 minutes right before our eyes on CNN.

I don't know about trying to sell the sport of sailing on television. I was at a fancy yachting party in Newport, Rhode Island some years ago, sitting there minding my own business, when Ted Turner came in with his team. The 12-meter races had been running on nationwide television, and they were all bragging that this was going to promote the sport of sailing and it was going to be the turning point ~ bigger than football, they said. Somebody finally asked me, "Old Savannah boy, what do you think about this idea?" I told him, "Sailing is an art. Like sex, it ain't a spectator's sport." I love sailing and do everything I can to get new people interested in riding the wind and getting food from the sea. I think this world we live in would be a much more peaceful and cleaner place if it was mandatory that everyone had to spend at least 2 months a year cruising on a 30-foot sailboat with their mother-in-law.

On the up side of 1995, the Miami sailboat show was one of the best yet, it appears that a lot of new people are getting into sailing and cruising. Multihulls are a big thing with all the modern conveniences on board. We have come a long way in the hundred years since Joshua Slocum sailed around the world by himself in a 38-foot wooden boat with only a compass, paper charts, sextant, an old clock with one hand, and no engine. I wonder what he would say if he came back now and saw all this modern stuff, carbon fiber masts, cellophane sails, glass hulls, winged keels, and especially electronic devices which tell us constantly where we are, not by the stars he used, but by our own stars we put up there ourselves. Electricity runs all of this using stored energy from the sun. Auto pilots are interfaced with GPS to tell us where to go. The auto pilots are also connected to radar and depth indicators so we don't run into anything along the way. Other conveniences include water makers and freeze dried foods, so we don't even have to stop along the way except to pick up some more rum.

This strange dichotomy leads to a delightful contrast you may encounter while cruising. You are likely to meet a couple who have a boat with a hand cranked diesel, oil lights and alcohol stove, and a manual pump for fresh water, and they will be traveling in company with another couple aboard a boat which has every electronic device you can imagine with a back up for each one. That's the beauty of cruising, we're all equal under the sun.

For my part, I am going to do my level best to give you the latest cruising news and useful tips to make life fun, safe, and comfortable while you are cruising and to get more people out on the water, young and younger alike. Look out! Nobody is safe.

Take my cousin Carole and her husband Jack; they have two little girls and a big house, and they both work. Carole works at a hospital and Jack is in the printing business. They started off small with a canoe and then a 20 footer. We showed them all of our pictures of snorkeling and diving and our videos of cruising trips we had taken to the Keys and Bahamas. They went to Florida a couple of times and got their deep diving certifications. I told my wife I was going to call Jack and Carole about a good deal on a 38 foot boat I knew about, at which point she said, "No way, they will never go for that." Then one of the doctors from the hospital took his family to the Bahamas on his 50 footer and raved about the wonderful time they had, which convinced my cousins to try it. One night the phone rang and it was Jack asking me about a 40 footer. I told my wife and she could hardly believe it. Jack said, "I'm really hooked now. I've got it bad, I've got to have twin diesels, a generator and an air conditioner."

Sure enough, they bought a 40 footer. It seems like a lot for a young family, but now when we see Carole, it's the focal point of their life, and is all she talks about. Jack is learning all about the maintenance and operation of the boat. Carole is learning about navigation. Their kids are being introduced to the great outdoors, and it gets them away from the TV and into catching and eating fish instead of grabbing fast food. Now I tell Jack, a boat is like a woman, you take care of her and she will take care of you. Never be in a hurry, don't spit into the wind, and don't sail where the trees grow.

My other cousin, Buddy, bought a large boat and uses it for entertaining guests for business and as a guest house when there are more visitors at his plantation.

SEA DOO ADVENTURE

My crew was part of the University of Illinois volleyball team which had come to Florida on spring break. We were sailing from Fort Lauderdale to Miami, about a mile off the beach, and then on over to Bimini for some partying. The women were enjoying the sun, and I had a couple of fishing rods running about 80 yards off the stern with 80 pound test line and two nice lures. I heard a buzzing noise and looked over to see two young men coming along on those Sea Doo water motorcycle things. They were headed so as to pass close off the stern. I suppose they'd seen the women on deck and were going to cut some capers around the boat. They were doing about 15 knots and would have hit those lines right about neck high. In my mind I said, "Look out for the hooks on the end there boys!" But in the real world I stepped back from behind the wheel and cut both the lines with my rigging knife just in time.

I waved to the Sea Dooers to come along side, then went down below and got a business card and a piece of masking tape. I stuck the card on the end of the boat hook and one of the women held it out for them to take as we sailed along.

"Okay, Dude," says I, "Jam this card down in your swimsuit there and send me 40 bucks when you get home to New Jersey or wherever for those lures and line I just had to cut loose." They didn't say much, as young gentlemen of the 90's are prone not to do. I guess they were in a daze that they had strayed out so far off shore, or mesmerized by my bikini clad crew. Anyway, I had forgotten to share this almost tragic event with my wife, who was greatly puzzled when I telephoned from the Bahamas about 3 weeks later. She said, "Are you selling fishing tackle these days?"

"Why?", says I.

"I don't know, but you got a check from New Jersey for 40 dollars and it says it's for fishing tackle. Thanks very much."

The moral of this story is if you're buzzing along on your personal water craft, watch out for that clear monofilament fishing line. It's very difficult to see unless you catch it just right in the sunlight. 'Cause hitting something like that at about 20 knots can ruin your day.

And if the two young gentlemen happen to read this column. Thanks for putting my faith back into the generation of the 90's.

A Hood 54 Ketch The "Tigeress".

THE PRAM FIRST BOAT

It was 1951 and I was eleven years old. My father had just died and his brother, my Uncle Hugh, to this day I'll never figure out why, sent off for a mail order 8-foot plywood kit boat, with 300 brass screws.

When it arrived, what a thrill that somebody would trust me with that much responsibility, ~ something I really didn't want to screw up on.

An unusual change not to be told, "Look out, be careful. You're going to mess up." I was careful on my own for the first time. The realization of this was like when I walked into the shed where I was working on the boat after school, I changed in my imagination from a pimple-faced eleven year old kid to a 6-foot tall boat builder with a red plaid shirt and blue overalls. I thought about the boat constantly and studied every detail. As my little vessel began to take shape I felt like I was creating something almost alive and why not! I started to think of its keel as a backbone, it had ribs like the human body and a plywood skin plus once she was launched into the water, I would be its brain and navigator. The boat would not be complete without me and, little did I know for the rest of my life, I would never be complete without a boat.

My Uncle Hugh would bring his friends around to see my progress. They would make mumbling comments about this and that but my instincts told me they only saw some plywood in the right shape. They didn't see the heart pumping in her little oaken keel. Uncle Hugh didn't see the magic in it either when he had to send a company carpenter over at great expense to take the window and sill out to get the "Sea Raven" out of the shed.

I painted the top sides a glossy black for my dead father, a white boat stripe for me, and a red bottom for the devil.

I was the only one at her launching party and celebrated with Coca-Cola and peanut butter crackers. She was a thing of beauty! I would lay in the grass in the breeze and just admire the grace of the way she sat on top of the water.

I cut lawns and raked leaves to purchase a set of 5-foot oars varnished with shiny copper tips and brown leather chafing guards. She handled like a dream, carried well with each stroke of the oars. When the wind was strong, I'd stand in the stern sheets, steer with an oar and she'd sail down wind. That's what she needed, wings to ride the wind. Again I think it was the first time I ever went to the library on my own accord ~ not for school work.

I noticed the library was really kind of a neat place with all of its hidden information. The enthusiasm of working on this project compared to something for school was 1,000 times more. I studied every kind of sailing rig you can imagine.

I guess my sincerity and enthusiasm was outboard where people could see it. Adults were much more helpful. The man at the lumber yard, the librarian, and the lady at the cloth store seemed to have a more sincere attitude in their helping and when my mother, after a hard day at work, was on her hands and knees on the front lawn helping me cut the sail with all the neighbors watching, I knew there was something positive about enthusiasm from the heart that was contagious, ~ like all these other people wanted a piece of the action.

When I sailed her the first time I thought of all of these folks who had helped me get her ready for this day when the "Sea Raven" and I would ride the wind like a bird. It was like they were all there, feeling the joy of one's first sail and they will always be there along with a lot more until the last sail.

AN UNEXPECTED BREEZE

I got a call from a broker right after New Year's to fly over to the Grand Bahama Islands and pick up a 50 foot motor sailor, *Marlin,* and bring her back to Fort Lauderdale. I could use the work, and it would give me a chance to try out the new cook on my charter boat. I called Wendy, she said she'd meet me at 10:00 at the airport the next day.

After checking the weather, I found nothing bad, but a cold snap could be expected. That meant taking along my heavy wool Irish Fisherman's sweater and lined rubber boots.

At the airport, the flight was at 11:00. No Wendy! I called her place, there was no answer. Well, tough for me, too late to get someone else, I guess I'll have to do it myself ~ it's only about a 20 hour run.

Flying over the Gulf Stream I could see a sailboat with all of her rags up, a tiny speck in the vast expanse of blue. I thought to myself, "I guess I'll be in that same spot pretty soon doing 5 knots with 800 fathoms of water under the keel ~ just me, alone.

When I arrived at the marina, I knew I was working for a good brokerage firm. The dock master had the keys, all bills were paid and she was full of fuel and water. *Marlin* was tied up in a slip about half way down the pier. She had nice lines with a high stern and a dinghy on davits. Down below was a lot of modern equipment for the times: generator, freezer, auto pilot. It looked like this delivery was going to be a snap.

About that time, my friend, Steve Herold, in port for a few days with a charter, hailed me. He didn't like the idea of single handing at night, but the *Marlin* had to be back in Fort

Lauderdale for a charter in two days.

It was 16:00 by the time Steve helped me cast off. Outside of the channel there was hardly any wind, I was looking forward to a calm crossing to America.

I raised the jib staysail, set the RPM'S on the engine at 1,200, put on the auto-pilot and went below for a cup of tea and a pizza which I had spotted in the freezer. What a life ~ crossing the Gulf Stream, eating a pizza.

Well, with the gentle roll of the boat, the drone of the generator and engine, and a full stomach, I dozed off. The next thing I knew ~ bump, bump, bump! I went up to the wheel to kill the throttle and realized that we were aground and it was dark!

I slowly got my bearings. Little Bahama Banks runs about 10 miles on the edge of the Gulf Stream north of Grand Bahama Island. On the starboard side I could see the lights of West End, about 5 miles away. In a fast analysis, I figured the limit switches had gone bad in the auto-pilot and we had made a long slow turn of 180° and run the *Marlin* back out on the Bahama Bank. I checked the tide tables in the Bahama Guide and it was on the way out. I could feel a little motion in the hull so I knew I was not too hard aground and that the boat was on sand. I went forward and got the plow anchor, pulled out lots of line on deck and took it back aft, outside of the rail and shroud so she was free to run forward when I rowed it out. I figured I'd put the plow in the dinghy, row out off the bow about 200 feet, drop the anchor and put the line on the windlass and kedge myself off before the tide left me high and dry. I put the anchor in the dinghy and lowered her down.

The double ended dinghy was suspended from the stern of the boat from the davits on each end. When I jumped into the dinghy from the high stern transom, I realized that I hadn't let her down far enough into the water. She turned over dumping me and my heavy lined rubber boots and fancy wool sweater into the chilly black water. The oars fell out, and the anchor got fouled up and was hanging down about 3 feet under the dinghy. To add to my predicament, I had left the staysail up.

What a time for a breeze to come up! I felt the *Marlin* heel slightly to port and she started to move. Ever so slowly at first then, bump, bump, bump and she was free. As she started moving faster the dinghy in her wake began to roll over and over. I was hanging on for all my life's worth with the plow anchor whacking me in the shins, my boots full of water and the soaked wool sweater weighed me down.

Looking up at the high transom stern, a picture flashed in my mind of the *Marlin* showing up in Palm Beach with no one aboard and me floating around in the water like shark bait. I started pulling and climbing, like a maniac, for what seemed like an hour.

When I finally got back to the deck of *Marlin,* the muscles in my arms were jerking and shaking with spasms. All I could do was lie there. As soon as I got my strength and my senses back, I was struck by the contrast of fighting for my life behind a boat that's sailing away and sailing peacefully along on a balmy Bahamian starry night. It will stick in my mind until the day I die.

We were back out in 16 feet of water, so I lowered and furled the stay sail and then eased the Danforth anchor down until it set. I hauled the dinghy back aboard, and got the plow anchor back in her chocks. Everything, at this point, seemed like it was moving in slow motion. After putting on dry duds, I had the urge to take a big shot of rum, but decided against it.

With the *Marlin* back under way again, I sat behind the wheel paying close attention all the way into Fort Lauderdale harbor. Other than some heavy ship traffic there were no more surprises that night.

At the Custom's dock, I found some diving gear aboard and went over the side to check the bottom of the boat for damage. Luckily, the hull looked fine. The following day, I stopped by the brokerage office to pick up my pay and expenses. After jawing awhile with John Cane, an English broker, he looked down and remarked "What a nice pair of sea boots. I must get a pair for myself'.

I replied, "I wouldn't, if I were you, these things could kill you if you don't pay attention. I almost had to call you from Freeport and say the boat was on the way. The only problem was, I was not on board.

Crossing gulfstream, 1963.

OLYMPIC SAILING SAVANNAH

We thought you would be interested in a report on Olympic sailing. Goodness knows, it was impossible to know there were sailing events from NBC'S non coverage; even the folks who put scores up on the Internet didn't seem to realize that the daily scores in sailing were necessary to follow the events.

I was there, and in talking with some of the Olympic sailors, I've never seen such dedication to any one subject. Years of practice every day, tuning the boat, the sails, reading the wind and water, then packing up loads of equipment, and taking the boat halfway around the world ~ what a spectacular event. You could feel the tension in the air, taste the emotion in the wind. We know they're the best in their countries. They came to see who was the best in the world. "Go for the gold," as Garry Hoyt wrote in the 70s, "remain focused", and that's what the 451 sailors from 68 different countries did riding the wind for speed and speed alone.

What a sight to catch a view of the Star class keel boats bearing down on the starting line, heeled over with the spray coming over their bows. And then, *bang!* We see the smoke from the starting gun, and they're off! All the years of practice comes to a head "right now." The keen eye of the helmsman shouts orders to his crew as his mind rushes to sum up all the knowledge gleaned from ancient mariners in his or her family's past. From the observation boat, I sensed them praying, "Come on baby, don't let me down now!" But only one can be the winner and when it crosses the line, there is no gray area. The elation of winning on the sailor's face is unmistakable.

It's legitimate pride. They paid their dues, and their fellow sailors acknowledged the fact. There was no envy or regret, as this reporter and sailor could observe ~ just respect and camaraderie, the sort a fellow sailor has for those who live their lives on the water.

The coast of Georgia was a great place to have the '96 sailing venue. They had some linguistic problems, but most of the foreign sailors I spoke with were amazed at the beauty of the coastline, and were amazed at the lack of development. They thought there would be marinas and condos everywhere.

Savannah had to build a floating marina to accommodate so many sailors out in the middle of nowhere. Fresh water to splash off the boats and competitors had to be ferried in barge loads.

Everyone was in a heightened state of awareness about the weather, because Hurricane Bertha had just buzzed off the coast with no damage there. That was just Mother Nature's way of keeping everyone on their toes. In fact, we had some southwest winds which seemed to give the sailors who hadn't had much practice on the courses an advantage.

The United States team won two medals: a bronze to woman sailor, Coutenay Beckar-Dey, and a bronze in the Soling Class for Jeff Madrigali, Kent Massey, and Jim Barton.

I think all the volunteers from Savannah should get a medal for showing such a great effort and perseverance in their many jobs: boat towing, land transportation, food, housing, banking, postal, medical and religious needs, not to mention entertainment.

For some reason, the people of Savannah thought the sailing Olympics would attract as many people as the celebration of St. Patrick's Day. It didn't. I guess they should have had a parade. Fiddlers in Thunderbolt said business was off and The Crab Shack, at Tybee, was about average. Savannah will go back to business as usual, a sleepy old southern city, and the sailors will get ready for Australia in 2000. God bless them all.

After the medals were awarded and the official remarks completed, Paul Henderson, president of the International Yacht Racing Union, quietly passed on the Olympic flag to Natasha Sturgen, the youngest member of the Australian team. With this simple gesture, he reminded everyone that Olympic Yachting will be back in 4 years ~ this time in the southern hemisphere in Sydney, Australia.

SAVANNAH YACHT & COUNTRY CLUB 1952
LISTS OF SAILING YACHTS

CLASS	OWNER	NO.	NAME
LIGHTNINGS	H.L. Backus, Jr	8	*Snark II*
	O.T. McIntosh &		
	James F. McIntosh	68	*Hurricane*
	S.Y. & C.C.	266	*Horsefly*
	Charlton Theus	801	*Skidaway*
	Spencer Helleckson	2089	*Hells' Bells*
	S.Y. & C.C.	2202	*Bubber*
PENGUINS	T. Turner	2796	*Black Cat*
	A. Moreno	2794	*Goofus*
	R. Gordon	2787	*Dottie*
	L. Thompson	2733	*Little Geech*
	N. McIntosh	2786	*Sal*
	E. Tosdal	2788	*Sea Bird*
	D. Scales	2790	*Imp*
	C. Helfrich	2793	*De Bunk*
	J. Kennard	2795	*Rebel*
	J. Morris	2864	
	F. Wahlstrom	2789	
	H. Strachan	2797	*Willie*
	J. Pinholster	2865	

EMERGENCY SAILING LESSONS

It was one of those rare nights when I stayed up past 11:00 and the phone rang about 11:10. It was a fellow named Jim Parker, he was calling from his cellular phone anchored off Key Louis in the Florida Keys. The connection was a little staticky and his voice was a little shaky. He said he had seen my ad in the Cruising Guide to the Florida Keys and that I taught sailing lessons. I assured him that I did but that I was booked until the following Thursday. He said he would like to book me as soon as possible. They had had two months of sailing lessons, but it didn't seem to have been enough. "We ran aground twice, tore a sail, had to get towed in, took a chunk out of the rubrail running into the dock, and last night we lost the cat overboard in a squall. My wife said this is the last straw. Can you help me?" he asked. I told him to leave his anchorage early tomorrow morning and lay a course for Key West. When you get a beam of Stock Island about twenty miles down yonder hail on channel 16 VHF for Southern Most Sailing, ask for Miss Robin. She will send out one of her employees in a dinghy to assist you in docking one of their slips at Ocean Side marina. Once you get tied up, they have a carpenter shop that will fix your rub rail and a sail loft to repair your sail. Ask Jeanne at the sail loft to make you up two heaving lines and two custom 10 foot aluminum boat hooks.

That will take care of the problems on your vessel. What about my other problems says Captain Parker. I mean, what would you do in my position? I don't know says I. I think take her out to eat at a fancy restaurant as soon as you tie up, check into a nice hotel for a couple of days, and do a lot of shopping, stop by the pound and pick up another pussy cat. I will be down Thursday, I need to know how many days you want instructions, I charge $200 a day any time from 1/2 day to 365 days I said jokingly. Captain Parker said how about ten days to start off with, it sounds like you know what you are doing. I called Robin to let her know there would be a novice on a Morgan 51' and to please give them some dock space.

I arrive Thursday morning bright and early to be greeted by smiling faces and a pretty little new cat named Bosun, a gray thing with little white feet. I loaded all my fishing gear and diving spears and we motored over to the shrimp boat piers to do some practice docking, they were amazed at how much help the ten foot boat hooks are, it gave them more confidence, all they had to do was get within 9-1/2 feet of the dock and pull in. It's a good advantage especially when there is no one to catch your lines on the dock and on a Morgan 51' they store easily on the forward cabin top along the handrails. I showed them how to use the heaving lines. We had them made out of polypropylene line that floats, it has a less tendency to get caught in the prop if you miss your throw. I also changed the dinghy painter to polypropylene and we put a couple of floats on that. They had a large Zodiac with a 25-horsepower motor, I rigged an old life jacket on the bow of the dinghy so it wouldn't scratch the hull and showed Mrs. Parker how to use it as a tugboat while going into a slip if wind catches the bow and starts to blow it over to the side, you can push it back in line with the Zodiac like a small tugboat. I explained to them as a professional skipper, many of times I have come into a crowded marina that I am unfamiliar with. I will tie up at the gas dock and walk over to see my assigned slip, check for the wind and the current. It takes a little extra time but it makes me feel a little more comfortable when I am operating a sailboat over 50 feet long and run into some strange wind and current that get you in trouble.

I have seen many a hot-dog skipper come in and get his bow caught into the wind, not being able to make his turn and rake the anchor down the topsides of some beautiful white powerboat. In the old days when that happened to a wooden boat, a little putty and paint and maybe the damage of $1,000. Now a days you scratch up the side of a big Hatteras with new two part epoxy paints and you are looking at a $10,000 repair job, so taking a little extra time and effort and planning can sure pay off in the long run. By this time it was about three o'clock so we went out for a little afternoon sail.

I noticed that in dropping the sails they had no problem with the mizzen, but the main was difficult. She had a big Bimini top and it was hard to furl and tie. The genoa furled okay but the braided dacron furling line was too large of a diameter for the spool, so I used an old trick I learned from Charlie Fowler, and when the line was furled up on the drum I took the core out of the braided line for the first 25 feet or so. You push the line together and pick the core out with a sail needle and cut it. Go down to the length you want, pick out the core again, pull it out, and now you've got a nice smaller diameter line to go on your furling spool.

This trick is slicker than goose grease on a door knob. When we got back to Ocean Side Marina I got Jeanne the Sail Maker lady to rig up some lazy jacks (small lines that come down just above the spreaders to the boom on each side to make dropping the main and mizzen sail much easier). After supper I took some pad eyes and hooks and ran a length of shock cord down the starboard side of the boom putting a pad eye about every 18 inches. Then in alternating spots I put the flat hooks on the port side of the boom, so when you drop the sails down in the lazy jacks, all you have to do is reach over and grab a length of shock cord, put it over the sail and hook it down continuing on down the boom, you have got that sail under control. It's a hell of a lot easier and faster than fooling with sail ties and once you get it adjusted right it will hold in a fair gale. The next day I showed Captain Parker how to talk to the commercial fishermen and shrimpers on the single side band radio to get a really good weather report. Who better to tell you about the wind and the water than somebody who has been fishing these latitudes for fifty years e'h?

While we were down below fooling around with the radios I sees that the galley is kind of sparse and the commadorable (Mrs. Parker) needs some more cheering up. This boat has a 110-volt generator available at all times, so the commodore and I slips over to Sears and come back with a microwave oven, toaster, blender (for rum drinks only), an electric can opener and a couple of nice 24" box fans to get some breeze flowing down below. The boat has an air conditioner but I likes the fresh air better and the boat ain't closed up all the time. It gets rid of that bilgy smell. This boat is 15 years old and I am sure that the bottom of those floor boards could tell some stories about what's been sloshed around on them if you let them.

Well, the commodorable was mighty tickled with her new galley toys. We conveniently neglected to tell her about the $700 worth of fishing gear we sneaked on the aft deck. That afternoon we headed out off shore for the first taste of blue water sailing, trolling with some ballyhoo (small baitfish) with two hooks rigged in it. We picked up two small dolphin and a nice sized kingfish. I made two rod holders out of two P.V.C. pipes and hose clamps, fastened them to a stantion on each side of the stern rail. I showed Captain Parker once you gaff the fish, take a squeeze bottle full of alcohol and shoot it down the fish's throat, it kills them instantly (maybe they go out with a buzz on). It keeps them from bloodying your poop deck so you are not trying to pop some big Kingfish in the head with a winch handle and end up losing it overboard. Most sailboat fishermen will tell you that 90% of the fish lost is after you get them on the deck.

I do love fresh fish on the grill with a little lime and pepper sauce, ride the wind and get your food from the sea, as the old Conch say the Lord will provide (we ain't polluting nothing) and that little new pussy cat was glad to see those fish too. Next was an anchoring lesson. I showed Captain Parker and the Commadorable as we call her now how to make anchor signals from the bow with your arms, port, starboard, ahead, neutral, etc., so you are not trying to yell back and forth against the wind, plus sound travels extra far over the water at a crowded anchorage and there ain't no sense letting the neighbors know all your business. We dropped the plow and set it with about 60 feet of road out, then we let the danforth down and let both anchors out about another 60 feet. I pulled out about another 40 feet on the danforth and left the line on the deck, then I showed them a foolproof anchor alarm.

I am sleeping in a bunk right under that forward cabin hatch, so before I go to sleep tonight I will run that extra line under the mattress in my bunk, so if she drags during the night it will pull that line out and wake me up. After some nice fish on the grill we told the commadorable to go down below and have a nice hot bath (this old Morgan 51' has a bathtub in the aft head and a water maker) and we will have a couple of cigars under the stars and do the dishes. I don't do dishes so I went and got my net diving gear bag, put all the dishes and silverwear in it, and hung it over the side until morning that works like a charm every time. Pull them up the next day, rinse them off with a little hot fresh water and you are on your way. The next class was on how to reef the sails. The weather was out of the Northeast at about twenty knots and overcast, not reafing weather for a Morgan 51', but a good atmosphere for it. We put up a stay sail with a reef in the main and the mizzen, the old girl was still making about 5 knots comfortably but not a bite on the fishing lines today.

We pulled into a little harbor behind Boca Grande, a small archipelago just East of the Marqueses. There were two other charter boats on the hook there, the Miki with Captain Scott on board, a local boat and the *Wandering Star* out of Palm Beach. I hailed them and told them we needed a lesson in rafting up. We put out two hooks in the middle of the harbor and Captain Parker and I divided the fenders up port and starboard. We took the *Wandering Star* on our starboard side. I showed Captain Parker when they were coming alongside, never have the masts side by side, always three or four feet forward or three or four feet aft, so if it gets rough or a big wake comes along, the spreaders won't hit or even worse than that get locked up together. I have seen that happen more than once.

We took the Miki on the port side. I introduced everyone and gave a little safety talk, don't sit and talk with your legs between the boats and whatever you do don't swim between them. These babies bump together and it will turn your head into jelly before you can say Ben Gun. A lobster fisherman came through the anchorage and Captain Dennis on the *Wandering Star* had made his acquaintance before. So after a lot of talk, a case of beer, and forty dollars cash we ended up with eighteen nice sized lobster tails. Then everybody went for a nice swim and some snorkeling. Supper was terrific, all the women pitched in with hors d'oeuvres and the men grilled the lobster. They were tucked behind that beautiful little island in the calm while the wind whistled and all the stars came out. Then us captains did our usual trick.

Dennis made up some rum punch and Captain Scott broke out his large deck speakers, put on some wild island music, and we all turned on our spreader lights. Everyone began to dance on the deck. Hell, I even danced with that little gray pussy cat. The moon came up and we all howled like wolves. When the spreader lights started getting dim, Mrs. Parker sat down beside me and said, "I didn't know this is what the cruising life is all about. We didn't need sailing lessons, we needed living lessons." It never ceases to amaze me that this magic still exists. I guess it will always be there as long as we have an unspoiled WIND and SEA to ride and harvest. Amen.

Boat Key, 1987, Marathon, Florida.

SCHOONER ON THE ST. JOHNS

Last November, we were delivering the 49 foot topmast schooner, *Ben Gun*, a lovely old wooden boat which the owner keeps in tip top shape. We had come down outside, around Cape Hatteras, and had gotten into some heavy weather. We rode the good winds as fast as we could, then ducked into Jacksonville for some sail repairs and to pick up some provisions. When I called the owner to report in, he said he and his family would like to join us for a sentimental trip down the St. Johns River.

After getting down the topmast, to allow clearance for a 45 foot bridge, and renting a 17 foot jolly boat with a 40 hp outboard, we picked up the owner's party at the Jacksonville airport and were on our way to Sanford, 150 miles up river. (Up, in this case means upstream, as the St. Johns is one of the few rivers in North America to flow northward.)

We had a fair breeze the first day, so we raised the sails as best we could with no topmast. It was quite a trip sailing through the port with its commercial activity, under the shadow of Jacksonville's impressive skyline. The river is quite wide, and we made it, under sail, all the way to Green Cove Springs before dark. We took a tour of the old navy base, where the confiscated drug boats are stored. There must have been 150 of all types – some with bullet holes. Man, if those boats could talk, I bet they'd have some wild tales to tell.

Our next port turned out to be the shooting location for a new Brook Shields movie to be called "Brenda Star." They had been on location up and down the river for several weeks, and the film crew we met gave us some good tips on places to visit and where to fish and gave us the name of a local fishing guide with the ominous name of Strangle Jack.

Not only did Strangle Jack find some great fishing holes, he introduced us to his niece who plays guitar and sings folk songs about the river, alligators, and all the characters up and down the shores.

It was nice to have live music while motoring along the river, but this put everyone on deck, restricting the helmsman's visibility. But, what the heck, a good time is worth a little inconvenience. The river really gets narrow where we were, and the girls on deck attracted a lot of attention; all the other boats wanted to come closer for a better look.

We also met an 80-year-old character called "Steamboat", whom we invited aboard for a drink. Steamboat said he used to work on the river boats carrying supplies up and down the St. Johns. He told us a lot of interesting history about the river during the Civil War and the Boom Days and offered to give us a tour of Blue Springs State Park. We made a trip through the dead river, Mud Creek, Blue Spring Run, Indian Hill... these are just the names I remember. With the owner's family, Steamboat, Strangler's niece and her guitar, a very large umbrella, and a picnic lunch, it was quite an adventure. The wildlife is fantastic. Piloting the jolly boat down those narrow creeks overgrown with large cypress trees, I felt like Humphrey Bogart on the African Queen.

PAPY'S KEYS

Written by the late Shilton Adams and Ann Readers
Charter's and Friends for Travel Magazine

＊＋ ❦ ＋＊

If you sail the Florida Keys, you'll see him one day. He'll be sitting in a laid back bar somewhere near the water, his beer belly stretching the buttons on a well worn, salt seasoned shirt. His sandy beard will be as unkempt and peppered with gray as his hair. On first glance you'll pass him off as a n'er do well, one more veteran of the army of cultural drop outs you always find in places like this. But if he catches your eye he'll ask you where you're in from. He'll ask you in that special way that sailors use as an invitation to talk about things nautical.

Before you know it you're sharing with him your full sailing history. And every place you've been he's been there, too. The boat talk will continue and as the ice melts in your drink, you'll notice something special about this man that you hadn't seen before. Maybe it'll be the sparkle in his eyes as he comments with a slow Savannah drawl on the itinerary you've just told him about. Maybe it'll be the soft, easy going manner that seems continually interested in where you've been and what you have seen there. It could be a joke he cracks with a Bahamian accent as authentic as any in Nassau, or a story of a passage so scary that it stops your heart. But whatever it is, when the conversation is finished you'll feel good about yourself, you'll feel good to be in the company of sailors like him.

Before you leave, you'll offer him your hand and tell him your name. He'll take it and shake it with a hand as big as a bear and with a smile as wide as the Gulfstream he'll say, "I'm Frank Papy." As you walk out of the bar the name will haunt you. You've heard that name before but you don't seem to be able to place it. Then, days later as you pull out the little book that has been your cruising bible and you check for the third time the approach to Mosher Channel, you'll see the name. "it's him," you'll cry out to your crew. "the guy in the bar. It's Frank Papy, the guy who wrote the book."

For thousands of people who have sailed the Keys, Frank Papy is the guy who wrote the book. His "Cruising Guide to the Florida Keys" has been the final authority on the tricky job of navigating the one hundred fifty mile stretch of archipelago that stretch south and west of mainland Florida. For over twenty years through his book Papy has kept "pilgrims" off the sand bars and coral reefs. He's detailed anchorages and warned about currents. He's outlined the best snorkeling spots and even furnished recipes on conch food from fritters to chowder. For thousands of Florida's sailors he has been the sailing equivalent of Dr. Spock, providing information that makes cruising these waters a far better and certainly less frightening experience.

But for all that he's done, his best lessons have gone untold. With the exception of those fortunate enough to spend a night or week or month in his company. The real guide to Frank Papy's Keys has yet to be shared, because for Papy the real Keys are much more than a place. They are a state of mind. They are the subtle combination of history and harmony. A place so spiritually removed from the mainland and the mainstream that it bears no resemblance to anything familiar. A world far different from any other place you have ever been before.

If I could grant one wish to all those soon to be Keys sailors, it would be to have the experience that I've had. To sail The Keys with Papy and hear the endless stories of the place he loves and knows so well, told in the voice of one of the last truly authentic sailors.

So sit back, pour yourself a rum punch and listen to the story of The Keys the way Papy would tell it if he were sitting in the cockpit next to you. If you listen carefully, you'll discover, as I have, a place so wonderfully exciting that you wonder how it still exists.

Good wind, warm weather, clear water, white sand, palm trees, fish, coconuts, fall of the trees, and it don't get cold. What do you want health care?

AMERICA'S OUT ISLANDS
SUBTROPICAL PARADISE YEAR AROUND

Imagine a cruising ground of 800 islands stretching across 200 miles of crystalline water, caressed the year-round by balmy southeast breezes. Add to this an abundance of rock lobster, fresh fish. crabs and shrimp, all yours for the taking. These are the main ingredients of America's Out Islands ~ the Florida Keys. If you live anywhere along the Eastern Seaboard and have the right boat, you can explore the only coral reef in the continental United States without ever having to make an open-water passage.

SAILING ROUTES
The Florida Keys separate the Atlantic Ocean from the Gulf of Mexico. There are basically three different routes you can take, depending upon the draft of your boat and how much you want to see.

Those with a maximum draft of 4-1/2 feet may sail the entire Gulf side, enjoy snorkeling, fishing, visiting marinas and resorts, and never be in water more than 15 feet deep. Because this route lies in the lee of the Keys, it is ideal for the beginning skipper with a family on board. The channels are well marked and there are no heavy swells for those who have a tendency toward mal de mer.

Hawk's Channel, on the Atlantic side, is navigable for boats drawing up to nine feet, yet is still partially protected by the Barrier Reef. Every year, more marinas open deep-draft facilities on the Atlantic side to accommodate a growing number of cruisers who are discovering the Keys.

The third route, for those returning home to Florida's east coast or beyond, is the Gulf Stream route, favored by blue water skippers for the 2 1/2-knot northeasterly current that can be a tremendous boost when weather conditions are right. The route is well marked with light towers for night navigation.

THE NORTHERN KEYS

You can mix and match these three routes to fit your boat's draft requirements, the weather, your sailing skill and schedule. Starting your cruise in the upper Keys with a sail down Biscayne Bay, I recommend trolling with a silver spoon. You'll probably pick up some fish by the time you make Elliott Key. And don't worry about hooking a porpoise; though they'll play in your bow wave, they won't take a hook.

Elliott is fantastic for beach combing on the Atlantic side. Because it is accessible only by boat, it is great for Picnicking on the beach. After overnighting here, head out Angel Fish Creek for some snorkeling on the reefs at John Pennycamp Coral Reef State Park. The coral formations and variety of fish are astounding. The treasure of the underwater park is the statue known as Christ of the Deep, located in about 20 feet of water. We always try to anchor so we're directly over it to surprise our cruising guests when they don their snorkeling gear and dive in. I keep a camera ready to catch their expression when they come up for air.

After a long day of diving, I like to anchor in Largo Sound or try one of the plush marinas in the Port Largo Canal. While ashore on Key Largo, don't miss the Koblic Marine Center with its underwater habitat and dolphins. If you arrive early enough or make a reservation ahead, you can swim in a lagoon with a school of porpoises.

You'll need at least two days of snorkeling the reefs in the park to see all the different types of coral formations and explore the wrecks. Two islands off Key Largo ~ Rodriguez and Tavernier Keys ~ offer convenient protected anchorages within a short sail of the best diving areas.

Below Key Largo lies Windley Key, one of our favorite spots. A large charter fishing flect ties up at the Holiday Isle Marina, so if you didn't catch any of your own fish, this is the place to buy it. Here you can meet some of the local characters. On the beach local musicians sing colorful songs about the history of the Keys, wild ladies, pirates and rum.

Just to the south are two government parks on Lignumvitae and Indian Keys. On Lignumvitae you can tour the tall groves of ironwood trees, Indian burial mounds and Spanish slave pens. This undeveloped island gives you an idea of how the Keys looked in pre-Colonial times.

On Indian Key you can explore the old ruins of a shipwreckers settlement. If you have youngsters in your crew, these islands are a must.

The next stop might be the city of Marathon on Vaca Key. As a major supply point, it is second in size only to Key West. There is an airstrip that is Perfect for crew changes. Two large marinas, Ferro Blanco on the Gulf side and the Sombrero Light House Marina on the Atlantic side, offer a full range of services. If you prefer to drop the hook among many live-aboards, Boot Key Harbor hosts a party onshore at the dockside bar every Friday afternoon. Everyone from the anchorage brings their supper ashore ~ it's quite a party.

THE LOWER KEYS

Marathon marks the beginning of the Seven-Mile Bridge, the longest in the world, connecting the northern Keys to the lower' Keys. This is the last crossover spot in the Keys, so if you intend to continue to Key West, you must decide at Marathon whether you want to travel on the Atlantic or Gulf side. Moser Channel has a new fixed span with a mast clearance of 65 feet.

Both routes from Marathon to Key West have advantages, depending upon the draft of your boat and the season of the Year. In summer, prevailing winds are east and southeast, so sailboats will get a better breeze on the Atlantic side. In winter. north and northwest winds can be strong, giving those who choose the Gulf side a screaming fast run. The third option is to take the Atlantic route, staying on the north side of Hawk's Channel to get some natural protection from the keys during northers and northeasters. My advice is to get a good weather report and choose the most comfortable route.

From here, the Keys take a more westerly direction, freeing the prevailing southeast winds for even better reaches.

En route to the next major port of call, Key West, be sure to stop for a dive at Looe Key. If you've chosen to sail the Gulf route to Key West, stop and explore some of the islands in the Big Spanish Channel.

Upon arrival at the main ship channel of Key West Harbor, you will see two convenient anchorages with dock space west of the city that are convenient to downtown and offer limited protection. The Galleon Marina has floating docks and is within walking distance of most of the attractions in the old city such as the Victorian Conch House, Sloppy Joe's Bar (a favorite hang out of Ernest Hemingway) and the James Audubon House with its beautiful renderings of birdlife you have seen on your sail down. Don't miss the gathering at Mallory docks to watch the sun melt into the Gulf. During the height of the winter season as many as 2,000 people gather for sunset celebrations that feature jugglers, fire-eaters, singers and dancers. You have never seen such carrying on.

About three days in Key West is enough time to sample the restaurants and take in all the history one can. After the big city life, it's fun to unwind in the unpopulated Marquesas Keys, 24 miles west of Key West. You can sail there in a day and land some fish along the way. The Marquesas' palm-lined sandy shores offer some of the best snorkeling around with plenty of wrecks to explore. Not far from here the infamous Mel Fisher discovered the wreck of the *Alshoa* with its millions in gold.

Forty miles southwest of the Marquesas Keys, across the open Gulf, lie the Dry Tortugas, an archipelago of seven islets that form the southernmost point of the eastern United States. This is a place you don't want to go without plenty of water, fuel, ice and extra supplies in case of delay due to weather or a mechanical breakdown.

Eighteen-century Fort Jefferson encompasses nearly all of Garden Key and what a sight to behold as it appears on the empty horizon. Once inside the harbor, there are several good anchorages. I recommend going ashore and asking the Park ranger which anchorage he recommends for the best protection. Among cruisers, Fort Jefferson is known as the Gibraltar of the South, a crossroads and turning point where you are sure to see someone you know. The fishing here is fantastic.

Now you've sailed the entire length of America's Out Islands. You've become acquainted with the "Conchs," as the native-born Keys residents are known, and sampled their food and music. On the return sail, try to explore those inviting spots you missed and catch your food from the sea. Remember the old conch expression: "Enjoy yourself. Today is not a dress rehearsal for tomorrow!"

The Morgan 41 goes
11 kn., 7 kn forward.
and 4 kn. sideways.
What a good old boat.

Sourell 48 air Bell

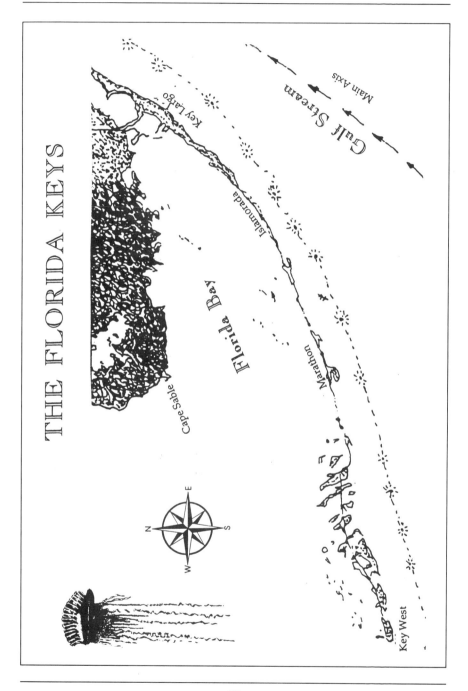

Nautilus CSY 44

It was my second week on the Nautilus, a CSY 44, what they call a walk-over model with the cockpit separating the aft cabin from the rest of the boat. It's a nice charter boat for college kids on spring break. When I checked the boat out, I noticed that the bilge pump discharge was only about an inch above the waterline, so I dug inside the hull to take a look at the hose. I did not like what I saw; there was no loop to prevent siphoning when the boat heeled over, but there was a large metal tube with the words "check valve" and an arrow pointing in the overboard direction. I had never seen a rig like that before, but I guessed it was okay. I checked the log book for any mention of trouble, and there was nothing in there about the bilge pump.

For this trip, there were seven young women from the University of Virginia aboard for a week's charter. We were heading out at 0600 for Bimini, and I asked my crew if they would make some sandwiches for lunch, because it was going to be kinda rough outside. They agreed, and got busy in the galley.

By noon I had a reef in the main with only a small club jib for a headsail. The CSY was hard to handle in the Gulf Stream seas, and she was bucking pretty well. I had a puke-factor of 50 per cent and one young lady, Jeenie, seemed quite scared.

I asked for someone to go down below and get me a sandwich, and one of them said, "There aren't any, we ate them all for breakfast."

"Oh," says I, and put the healthiest looking of my charges on the helm, telling her to just hold it. I would direct her from below by yelling, "a little left" or "a little right", while I made some grub. While below, I took the opportunity to turn on the bilge pump and check the course. I made some sandwiches, turned off the bilge pump, and went back on deck. It was getting rougher, and we had about another 5 hours to go.

I went below again about 10 minutes later, and ~ holy moley ~ there was water a couple of inches over the floorboards. I called one of the boats we were sailing with to let them know we had an emergency and asked them to stand by. I switched the bilge pump on manual and raced through the cockpit down into the aft cabin to see if I could tell where the water was coming from. When I came back through the cockpit, the scared one, Jeenie, was in a panic and was having difficulty breathing. One woman said, "Captain, what do we do?"

"I'm really busy right now", I replied. "Everybody give her a hug."

When I got back to the main cabin, the water level appeared to have stabilized. Maybe it was a little lower, so I went back on deck to check on my passengers.

They were all over Jeenie, hugging her, and she was yelling, "Get off! You are squashing me." She had switched from being scared to being mad.

I got everybody calmed down and radioed the other boat that we are okay. Sure enough, it had been the check valve. When I had turned it on while below making lunch, the check valve had become stuck open and water came back into the boat. When I turned it off this time, I luffed the boat up so that the outlet was above the waterline and she was okay.

Some people will spend $200,000 on a boat and put in a bilge pump that isn't big enough to circulate water in a small bait well. I like to have two electric pumps above waterline with automatic switches and an alarm on the one set the highest; a hand pump with the pump handle at the helm. If you have to pump and are singlehanding, you can steer and pump at the same time. In a lot of new boats the hand pump is down below somewhere. Not good I am a firm believer that you should be able to pump the bilge, start and stop the engine, talk on the radio, and control all sheets without leaving the steering station, be it tiller or wheel.

That's one of the few points my fellow charter captains will not argue with me about. The subject seems so simple: water comes in, you get it out. On my charter boat I start with two buckets aft with 6-foot lanyards tied to the bails. I like the rectangular plastic buckets with a good metal handle. The top bucket measures 6 inches by 14 inches and is 18 inches deep. Half way up the lanyard is a brass snap. There are rings on either side of the stern rail, so when you are finished with the bucket, you just snap her to the ring and she's neatly upright. Inside on the bottom of one of the buckets is written "puke here." In the other one it says "half-way." Charterers always ask, "Half-way, what's that?" I say, "When you lose that one half way through the trip, we finish with this one." Nobody ever pukes in the first bucket.

I like the rectangular size because it's easy to use for bailing, getting into tight spots. When scooping up water from over the side while under way, you throw the square bucket with a corner down, and it scoops and fills better and faster than a round-ended bucket. If it gets loose on deck, it won't roll overboard.

For a hand bilge pump, I prefer one with the handle you draw straight up, so you can feel the suction with every stroke. Mine has a y-valve with two hoses leading into the bilge, each with 4-inch high heavy metal strainers. If one hose gets plugged, you switch the y-valve and keep pumping while another crew member cleans the plugged hose.

Electric bilge pumps must be mounted where they arc accessible so you can work on them easily and clean the strainers. They should be at least 2 feet above the waterline. We use the flapper-valve type automatic switch. They are easily tested by just lifting them. Use stiff, reinforced hose, which won't collapse under suction, and double stainless steel hose clamps. Make sure the hose has a smooth texture on the inside to prevent sludge build-up. Try to have as few sharp bends as possible, and use 90-degree elbows. I like to have the bilge pump wired directly to the battery, so you can't turn the automatic bilge pump off accidentally and you can turn off the master battery switch without disabling the automatic bilge pump.

For an emergency pump, you can install a belt-driven pump with a manual clutch off the main engine.

Here is a rule of thumb we old charter captains use for a 30 foot boat: a 1-inch hole, 2 inches below the waterline will let in 3,500 gallons of sea water in an hour. You've got to stay ahead of the game.

Every now and then, you should go down into the bilge on a treasure hunt. You will be able to eliminate lots of junk that will clog your pumps, and you will find old tools, nuts and bolts, pens ~ all sorts of stuff ~ not to mention that cleaning the bilge a bit will make it fresher smelling. There are a lot of biodegradable bilge cleaners available these days, but I haven't found a rum-scented one yet.

"The waters I said are deep. Who knows the many secrets they keep."

Spring break college girls.

Good sea boat,
CSY 44 1981.

A STRANGE AMERICAN CUSTOM

I will tell you that time does fly, it was another spring break college season and I had another eight weeks of student charter back to back; that means coming in on Friday night, loading up and leaving on Saturday afternoon. I was into the fifth week and getting tired. We had a group of six boats this particular trip: five Morgan 41 sailboats and an Irwin 42 with a total of 35 students from a college in Ohio. I was the only paid professional Captain in the group, the rest of the skippers were from the school's sailing club.

We loaded up in Ft. Lauderdale and headed across the Gulfstream to Bimini, Bahamas. To the dismay and displeasure of the students, it rained and blew out of the Northwest really hard for two days. Being stuck at the dock in Bimini, the kids were really getting antsy. So, the other five college boy skippers and I decided we would sail them up to West End Grand Bahama for some fishing and diving. We checked the weather forecast and it looked good for the next morning. We decided we would depart Bimini around 4:30 a.m. but we were a little late getting away because we forgot about rounding up the crew, chasing them off the beach and out of the bars. I guess it was around 5:00 a.m. before we got out of Bimini and headed North up toward Great Isic Light. This is one of my favorite fishing ground and sure enough we picked up two nice dolphins and a small tuna.

We caught sight of the landfall of Grand Bahama Island around 11:30 and by 3:00 in the afternoon we were anchored in the little cove just outside the "Jack Tar Marina" at West End for a swim and to get these wild kids organized for a docking without any mishaps. I took the dinghy in and walked over to the Marina to see the dock master. He had six slips he could put us in together on the eastern side of the Marina, so as not to disturb the more conservative yachtsmen on the western side of the cove with these boisterous youngsters. I went back on board, informed the other skippers of our arrangement and we all got our hooks up and headed into the Marina.

As we were coming in, I noticed some commotion and saw five or six gentlemen running down the dock to help us tie up and some ladies on the other side of the marina pointing skyward. It seems that one of the boats had talked one of the lady crew members into removing her bikini top and had hauled her up the mast in a bosoms chair. This is a heck of a way to enter a harbor and it seemed to get a lot of people's attention and their help in getting us tied up. I guess that is not so bad.

We finally settled in, had a cook-out on the little beach behind the boats that night. The dolphin charcoaled on the grill was fantastic.

The head organizer of the trip had made arrangements to transport all 35 of his colleagues to Freeport the next morning so the kids could get a look at the town and visit the casinos. I was invited to go, but declined after meeting some old sailing friends at the dock. We planned a dinghy trip over to Indian Cay for some diving and a picnic. The next morning after breakfast, I saw them mixing up a concoction they call purple passion which they intended to take to Freeport with them. They had two five gallon plastic water coolers for containers and they were pouring numerous quarts of Vodka, Rum and Bourbon, mixed with canned fruit juice. After seeing that, I was glad I decided to stay for my picnic.

It seems that the transportation they had arranged for was

late and while they were waiting they started sampling their brew. Finally, after quite a wait, a giant old yellow school bus arrived and they departed laughing and singing.

The weather was nice after the rain in Bimini and we had an enjoyable lunch and snorkeling trip. When we returned to the marina around 4:00 p.m. and I had just gotten the gear unloaded out of the dinghy when my old friend Richard, the day shift dock master, said "Hey Captain Frank, the Constable from Settlement Point be wanting to see you and mighty quick up in de office." Sure enough, up in Richard's office was this tall Bahamian sitting in his white uniform with all sorts of belts and badge and a white pith helmet. He looked like one of those policemen you see directing traffic in Nassau on all the postcard and posters. Trained in strict British Customs, he snapped to attention when I entered the office and asked me if I was in charge of these college people? I informed him that I was the only professional Captain in the fleet of six boats and the other skippers were college students with sailing experience however, they were unfamiliar with the waters of his beautiful Bahama Islands; I was there as their guide so to speak.

"What's the problem" I asked.

"Problem" he said, and went into a restrained British rage dropping back into his Bahamian accent when his emotions got the best of him. "What are dees people anyway! Some kind of perverts or somethin', indecent, I say! pressing their bare buttocks up against the glass window in de bus. Boys and girls alike shocking my Bahamian brothers and sisters to no end and causing traffic to back up and almost a car crash.

Well, after a quick mental analysis it seems with the bus being late, the kids were well oiled with the booze and about half-way to Freeport the bus broke down. The driver wouldn't let them off in their inebriated state fearing they would get run over in the highway traffic, so in retaliation they started "mooning" the cars going by forgetting they were in a foreign country. As a result, they had been arrested for indecent exposure and were in the Settlement Point jail house about a mile away. I've seen the place and I couldn't picture thirty-five American college students in it but, I guess it was true. The Constable saw me pondering, looked me in the eye and asked me: "You're an American citizen, what is the significance of this here action?"

I replied "The only thing I can say is that it is a strange American custom among college students."

"Well, what am I gonna do now?" he sighed.

"We're leaving in the morning, so why don't you fine all of them $10 a piece and release them in my custody and I'll see that they behave until we leave," I offered.

The Constable and my good friend, Richard the dock master, had a private conference about my character and judgment.

"Being as you a sailin' captain in high regard, I'll agree." he said.

So we proceeded to the small jail house where my motley crew was most pleased to see me. The news of their release increased my popularity tremendously. They paid their fines one by one and I assembled them in a group like soldiers outside the small jail house. The Constable was very impressed with their humility and obedience. We said our good-byes and I proceeded to march them in a quiet formation through the little town... hup 2, 3, 4, hup 2, 3, 4, right turn march.

Out of the corner of my eye I noticed some Bahamian villagers coming out to watch and smiling shyly as we passed through town on our way to the Marina.

We paid up our dockage, including a large tip and thanked

Richard for his help and confidence.

Darkness was coming on soon so we sailed back out to the small harbor and set the anchors for the night. The kids took the dinghies ashore for a cookout that began quietly and progressed to their old selves again ~ drinking, loud music and generally having a ball ~ getting it out of their systems so they could go back to their work and studies 'til next year's spring break charter.

FISHING FROM A SAILBOAT

They say fish is brain food. I try to eat it every chance I get, but I don't think it is doing any good. The older I get the less I know, but I do know that good fresh fish is about $6.00 a pound, so when I am sailing I always troll a couple of lines off the stern. We use a rod and reel whenever possible, but when flying into some foreign port in a tiny charter aircraft, I carry about 600 feet of 100-pound test line, hooks, leaders and a few lures, and a piece of shock cord rigged into the hand line so it won't be such a jolt when the fish hits. I make a gaff hook out of an old mop or broom handle, using two hose clamps and an extra large hook. A pair of white cotton gloves comes in handy for pulling in the line. I use a squirt bottle full of rubbing alcohol to shoot down the fishes throat so they die instantly ~ I hope with a buzz on. This keeps us from blooding up the deck and lets you get the hook out and back into the water as soon as possible, especially when you are in a school of fish. I have gotten as many as a dozen mahi mahi in 30 minutes. Usually, we eat some, put some on ice, and have been known to swap eight nice fish for dockage or two nights eating and drinking at a local restaurant. But most of the time after the first night at the restaurant I'm limited to just eating, if you get my drift.

In my years of delivery work I have developed the reputation that: if you sail for Papy you will always have fresh fish. It helps nowadays with good crew hard to find.

I ran a flotilla charter a few years ago down in Tortola, I managed to feed seven boatloads of folks mostly fish for 5 of the 8 days we were out, it turned out to be a great bonus, my wife and I got all of the leftover food.

Sometimes on a big ketch I will run a small block and line up to the top of the mizzen so I can haul a clothes pin up, I put the line from the rod into the clothes pin, run it up to the top of the mast so when the fish hits it pops out. The advantage is when the boat rolls under sail it makes the bait move from side to side. The fish seem to love it. I figure it increases your odds of catching fish about 20 percent.

Part of the reason I love my job is to pull in a couple of 3-foot mahi mahis, dolphin not Flipper, to my charters amazement. I gaff them give them the alcohol treatment lay them out on the aft deck and have my picture taken skinning and filleting these beauties while having a rum and coke on a sunny day with some Jimmy Buffet music on the tape. I cook them up for lunch with some butter, lime, and pepper sauce ~ all done by me on a rocking boat, unless I have the luxury of having a cook on board. The log book usually reads, two fish on board at 10:30, lunch at 12:00, six charterers and the captain ate 12 pounds of fish fillets and 12 more pounds are in the cooler.

Fishing from a sailing vessel is ideal as there's no prop wash or disturbance in the water so you can run your bait closer to the boat, and a good trolling speed is from 3 to 8 knots. You don't have to worry about the speed. Deep water fish don't eat with a knife and fork, they come in at 40 miles an hour.

Here is a story of catching a white marlin from my Morgan 41 charter boat which goes 11 knots ~ 7 knots forward and 4 knots side ways.

While sailing I always troll a couple of fishing lines off the stern to pick up some mackerel or dolphin. It breaks the routine for the charterers when we get a strike. I tell them, ride the wind and get your food from the sea. But fishing from a sailboat is hard. The power boaters figure sailors are too lazy to fish so they come close off your stern and cut your lines. So you must use economic methods. Because I lose so much gear, I got my rods and reels at Sailorman used marine store, and I get my line and lures at the flea market. When I leave the States with a more affluent charter I can usually talk them into buying a half a dozen rigged ballyhoos for crossing the Gulf Stream.

Well, the fishing action on this particular charter was a family of four from mid-Florida. The mother was a real character. She had called me before the charter and asked about the boat hijacking and pirates. She said her husband was kind of a wimp and she didn't know what sort of guns she should bring. I assured her we had arms aboard and there was nothing to worry about. She had a drinking problem and was getting ready to go into AA for treatment and the daughter had just gotten out of a drug rehabilitation clinic. The son was 14 years old, about six-two, and due to his size and age ratio had a coordination problem. The father was about 50 and said he was prone to getting seasick. They were dead set for going to the Bahamas even though the weather looked a little sloppy. The mother and daughter had taken a half dozen Dramamine between them, chased down by a couple of glasses of gin, and went to sleep in the aft cabin double bunk.

We started about 8 in the morning, crossing the Gulf Stream, motor sailing in about a 10 to 12 knot wind and a lot of rain squalls around with Mr. P and I taking turns at the wheel. I was running a fishing line off the starboard rail with my biggest sea rig and my one and only ballyhoo left over from the last charter. We were about 15 miles west of Bimini when a white marlin struck. I raced back, grabbed the rod and set the hook. The marlin jumped for the second time and then I gave the rod to Mr. P who didn't reel in fast enough and the next time the fish jumped it looked like the line was wrapped all around him.

I suggested that the boy get the camera because I didn't think we were going to get him in now, but we could at least get a picture of him if he jumped again.

Well, it appeared that the fish went straight down, sounding I think they call it, and it must have straightened out all the line. Mr. P sat down on the deck with a cushion between his legs and after about 12 minutes was saying, "Hey bud, you said I couldn't get him in and how are you going to get him on this boat?"

I had never boated a billfish of any kind before but I had seen it done. I remember a gloved hand on his bill and a gaff in the other hand. The gaff hook I had on board was fairly small and the only glove I had was an electrician's hot wire glove I used for diving (it's heavy rubber and comes up almost to the elbow). Now, I figured if I got on deck there was no way I could put him in the cockpit; it is in the middle of the boat and we were rolling pretty good. To keep a slippery fish as heavy as that on a rounded deck was going to be a problem, so I told the boy to squat down with a slip-knotted line, to loop it around the fish's tail if I got him on deck, and tie it up short on the stern cleat. I had left the mizzen up and sheeted in tight to reduce the rolling. I got the glove and the gaff and I stuck a heavy winch handle in my belt. I figured to gaff the marlin two or three times to take some of the fight out of him before I got that monster on the deck. Well, I did and he was red hot. Blood went everywhere on me, on the deck, even up on the mizzen sail. I got a hold of his bill and lifted him up with the gaff. The boat took a heavy roll and I managed to get him on the deck. I didn't realize that they had a bottom bill. I felt a sting and looked down and the lower jaw bill had cut right through my glove at the wrist, what then? Oh well, no time for that now. The fish made another lunge and we both went down on the deck with me on top. The boat took another roll and we started to slide but believe it or not, the kid had gotten the line around the fish's tail and tied it up short to keep us on the deck. I braced myself and started using my worst language on the fish. I took the winch handle out and gave this 7-foot, 92-pound white Marlin a wrap on the head. As I raised up to give him another wrap, for good measure, something caught my eye.

All this had been going on right over the aft cabin and woke the mother and daughter. Hearing me cussing and swearing, not knowing we had a fish, they figured I was after her husband or son. Seeing all the blood around and presuming she was next to be victimized by this pirate, she had armed herself with a derringer ~ and that's what had caught my eye. Luckily the boat was rolling and the mother was too drugged to hold her balance. Mr. P. grabbed the gun away from his wife and explained to her that it was a fish and fish blood. I apologized for my language, but I had gotten mad at the fish who had cut through my glove (luckily it wasn't a deep cut).

So we hung the marlin from the mizzen and motored into the "Big Game" club at Bimini. We put him on the scales and Mr. P. made arrangements to have it mounted. They'd just had a fishing tournament at the club and there were still a lot of boats that had not gone home yet, so we attracted quite a bit of attention.

That night we went out to the Compleat Angler Bar. I was sitting there talking to some friends when I noticed four or five powerboat types gathered around. You can recognize them easily: They wear khaki's and a khaki hat with a bill on each end and a knife and pliers and all sorts of things on their belt. They all came over to me in a group and asked, "Are you the rag merchant (that's what powerboats call us sailboaters) that brought in the big white?" In their special jargon they wanted to know what method I used to get him up to bite. I tried to look as serious as I could and said, "I went, 'Here fishy, fishy fishy…'" which they took as a joke, and we all had a round of rum.

92 pound White Marlin on the Nautica, caught with rod from Leicester Hemmingway.

SPRING BREAK ON A SAILBOAT

I came back from a charter last month skylarking around the Bahamas. When we got back to the dock my wife asked one of the ladies in her early forties did you have a good time? And, did the Captain behave himself? She replied, "great time", and thought for a minute, "The Captain is, the most responsible man I ever met in the most immature way!" Overhearing this I was stunned by her remark. My wife answered casually, "Oh that's because he has been taking college charters out for the last 16 years, when they come down on their "Spring break." I never really thought about it, but I guess she is right. At 45 years old, most of my contemporaries think the Police are someone who arrests you and the B52 is a big airplane instead of two rock bands.

Spring break for the schools starts around the middle of February. Out Island charters in Miami was my first introduction to college charters. Eight forty-foot sailboats with skippers, fifty college kids, 120 cases of beer, lots of bread and balogna, and we all set out for Bimini for a week. What a blast. The music goes on night and day. When they first came aboard, I was a little worried about them tearing up my boat, but all and all they behaved pretty well.

Six of them aboard the boat from the University of N.C. four girls and two boys. They didn't dirty any dishes the whole trip. They ate over the sink, a bite of balogna, a bite of bread, a bite of cheese, and a swig of beer, and they are always in a hurry. It seems that they want to do everything at the same time, to have as much fun in as short of time as possible. Here in the tropics where there are no real seasons of the year, that's the way most charter captains keep track of the date, "Hey man you mean it's spring break time already." Time really flies when it's summer all these days. Year before last on the third week in March we had twenty-six boats, just one company. We boarded and disembarked at the Miami Marina, the only place really big enough to handle that many transient boats, and cars, etc. Hodge Gallop, the dock master there, was a great help; there were sixteen boats and Captains waiting to be loaded and go out, and I was in the Bahamas on a forty-six footer with nine other boats coming back with the previous week's group. We get in about 10 p.m. Friday night and leave about 4 p.m. Saturday afternoon. That's a short time, but by 3:30 p.m. Saturday we had all the boats but two, loaded and out with ice food, drinks, wind surfers, snorkeling gear and lots of suntan lotion. It cost each kid about $400 a piece for the boat, Captain and food; but no drink, they have to supply that. Most of them say it's cheaper to go sailing than to lay around Ft. Lauderdale in a hotel and buy their food and booze at bars and restaurants.

We cross the Gulf Stream and anchor behind Gun Cay. If it's rough we call the flotilla, "the puke pack." I have seen them throw up in my compass, my rubber boots, and in the sink. Sometimes it's so bad we have to assign barf buddies, someone to help you when you are sick.

The next morning, it's a beautiful sight, all the boats anchored and the kids swimming and having breakfast of beer and corn flakes, the colorful sails of the wind surfers zipping in and out among the anchored boats. After breakfast we usually split up the boats into two groups. I take half up to Bimini to clear customs and Captain Eddy Aguara who runs the company takes the rest into Cat Cay to clear, due to the limited customs personnel at both ports.

After a nice sail into the harbor and dockings, the fun starts:

music and dancing, limbo contests and generally partying day and night on the dock. The more organized crews are cooking out on the grills and the less organized are eating over the sink. When the other boats arrive from Cat Cay we have enough people and boats to cause inflation in Bimini. I must compliment the people of Bimini and Cat Cay for putting up with the frivolity and antics all done in good fun.

There is a great camaraderie among the charter sailboat Captains and this gives us a good chance to catch up on the news of what each other has been doing over the year. It's kind of a reunion and party for us too, while working. We have three lady sailboat Captains in the group now, which really helps in the activities, especially in the communication department, having usually a larger ratio of girls on board, where as before if a girl had a problem sometimes it was difficult for her to discuss this with her male Captain. We sort of take turns keeping an eye on the boats and our wild and crazy passengers, helping them rig up dinghy races, wind surfing races, diving and sailing trips.

We make Bimini the unofficial headquarters taking day and overnight sails down to the beautiful beaches and reefs of Gun and Cat Cay, with some of the boats even going up to Freeport for the more affluent kids who want to gamble.

We work it out among the Captains who want to stay in port, who want to sail or dive, etc. When I am at the dock in Bimini, I usually get up around 8:00 o'clock, check the boats and walk over to the beach for a swim. I have seen "radio beach" look like after a World War I battle, all the kids sleeping or past out in the sand with beer cans and rum bottles scattered everywhere. Captain Dick Karr is usually in charge of assigning different boat crews to take turns cleaning up the beach the following day.

On the day before we leave weather permitting the owner of the Compleat Angler Hotel throws a wet t-shirt contest and party for the kids and a free night at the hotel for the winner of the wet t-shirt contest. One of the games consists of smashing a coconut on the ground until it breaks open. I think there is a lot of skill in it because usually a small Bahamian can open it before some giant football jock can, much to the amazement of the judges who get free drinks and can't figure out much of anything after a couple of cups of grogg.

The next day we depart back for America. It's a mad house getting ready, trying to find the gear and clean up with the bad hangovers. We were having oranges in the cockpit when one of my crew came up with some aspirin. I told her, "Let me know if you feel better!" "Why?" says she. "Because you just took two orange seeds instead of your aspirin!" To which she replied, "Awesome! Far out! Like wow! I am such a geek!"

Each year the Captains have to learn a whole new language or at least we think we do, say for example "to be seasick: barf, flash, buick, ralph, toss your cookies, dump your lunch, bif, puke, chunder and up-chuck. This talk doesn't seem to bother the Bahamians, they have a language all their own. The only thing that seems to baffle the Bahamians is the strange American custom of "mooning."

I think they take it too literally.

If we are lucky on the sail back, we will get a fifteen to eighteen knot southerly wind. We all sail back together. It's quite a sight, about 3 dozen or so boats waiting to get started back for another load.

A good broad reach across the gulf stream always seems to rejuvenate my spirit. The freshening wind clears the air, and cobwebs out of my brain; and the sea spray washes off the boat. Usually the crew is sleeping off hangovers and getting rested for their long drive back to school. The quiet after all the noise and chatter seems strange.

When we arrive at the dock in Miami some of the new group are in already, lots of good-byes and we will be back next year. Many of them keep coming back. I have some repeat charters that I originally met on their spring break. They bring their family with them now, trying to recapture the sweet kind of youth. They say it's not quite as much fun as the first time, but they haven't found anything to beat it yet. Girls, sailing, rum, gin, and dancing, sometimes I think we never grow up, we just grow older.

Earnest Hemmingway's brother, Leicester, in Bimini.

"There are many other ways to lose your life other than death."

My mate, Nora Papy.

Christ under water in the The Keys.

"There are many other ways to lose your life other than death."

Ohio girls, "Whitey and what's her name".

A shirt from my favorite marine store in Ft. Lauderdale.

"There are many other ways to lose your life other than death."

Sea planes at Dry Tortugas.

Jerry in Bimini, couldn't read or write, but one of the smartest people I have ever met.

SKYBIRD, THE TEST BOAT

Here are some interesting experiences that happened on board while cruising the *Skybird*, a 1967 Morgan 34-foot sloop which is doing well, testing new products which are being sent to me. She has a lot of age on her, but my wife says "she sails like butter."

The latest thing we are testing is a jaw-type jam cleat on the roller furling line with which we unroll and roll up the jib. We first saw this cleat on another Morgan 34, Felicity, owned by Captain John Lee. The cleat is handy when you are furling the sail and have to change your grip on the line or, it's too hard to get the line in the rest of the way. You simply drop the line down in the jam cleat to hold it temporarily. So far, it's working great. We suggest installing a jam cleat on the cockpit coaming with the lead in line to the furler with nothing in the way to divert it. This surely beats trying to take a couple of turns around a conventional cleat when there's a strain on the furling line.

Our next concern was blisters in the fiberglass hulls of older boats. We've been asking others how they cope with the problem. We heard a comment while anchored down in Georgetown, in the Exumas, from a couple with an old Pearson 35. We'd been discussing hauling our boats while watching the crew of a little 30-foot sailboat painting her bottom while lying on her side on the beach at low tide. I commented that if they found any blisters, they wouldn't be able to repair them before the tide returned.

The couple from the Pearson said they had found about a dozen blisters on the hull over a period of about 15 years. They check them every time they haul out to see if they are any larger and if not, simply leave them alone. Generally, the fiberglass on these older boats is so thick that blisters don't seem to matter. Jokingly, the captain said, "they might slow the boat down a little but, then again, they might speed it up: "look at all those bumps on a golf ball which makes it fly farther."

We took the dinghy over to where the owner of the 30-footer was painting like mad to beat the incoming tide, and engaged him in conversation as he painted. He said he was getting even for the $100 charged by the Bahamian Government for a cruising permit this year and calling that his "yard bill" for the year.

It used to be free to come to the Bahamas and get a cruising permit for 6-months, then it cost $10, then $20, and now $100 with a $25 fee for each person aboard more than two. I talked with another skipper later on that week who had three couples aboard when they cleared into Cat Cay. He said he had been charged $25 to tie up and $175 to clear customs. The crew got a little upset at this high price, so the Bahamian Customs officer said that included a fishing license. When the crew said they didn't fish and didn't eat fish, the customs man turned and left, saying, "Have a nice day."

The price of rum is still cheaper in Bimini and the crew of the Skybird can usually be found at the Complete Angler bar owned by the late Ozzie Brown. What a terrific guy he was. He used to let me be the relief player on the congo drums in the band.

CAT ON A BUDGET

The sun was just an orange ball with the morning haze slowly being burned off by another new day. The anchorage had been quiet during the night. We hadn't heard the weather report yet, but if we got a favorable breeze we would make for Charleston, or somewhere, today. We had no place to go, and all day to get there, cruising with some old friends who have a 40 foot Catamaran. It's a great lifestyle.

We're all on a tight budget these days, but we've been catching plenty of fish. Bill and Kelly had been charterers with me 9 or 10 years ago. They liked it so much, they decided to get their own boat. They had been looking at catamarans but were shocked at the difference in the price, between a half a cat and a full cat (a trimaran being a cat-and-a-half). A brand new fully equipped French catamaran was close to a quarter of a million dollars. They had looked at some used ones, which were awfully beat up, and even those were about a hundred thousand. They were just about ready to throw in the towel when a mutual friend told me of their problem. We had given them a hail on the land line and spread out a plan for this couple that I had always had in the stern of my coconut (back of my mind). After delivering a couple of cats from St. Thomas I became interested in that style of vessel. A broker friend of mine had told me there was an abandoned Wharram cat on a vacant lot off the Intracoastal Waterway on Miami Beach, and I'd had a look at it late one afternoon. Compared with all the boxy cats I'd seen, this one had a fair looking cut to her hulls. She was in rough shape, the decks were rotten, and the mast was missing. In researching this endeavor (bar talk) I had found the buzz words of multihulls were "strong" and "light." That was one of the reasons they are so pricey. Well, having a too-long-in-the-tropics brain, I figured they meant light pole as in street light. You see lots of them lying around the aluminum scrap yards. I devised a plan of using the old hulls as a pattern, and to tap the resources of a talented Cuban carpenter and welding craftsman I knew, named Vince, and the most unbelievable resources of used material you see around. I consulted Vince, about this project, and it took about a week for him to give me his report. Using the old hulls as pattern, Vince said he could duplicate the hulls in marine plywood, with a thin coat of fiberglass, for $3,800. I suggested, joining the two hulls with aluminum street light poles. They're perfect for the job. With a ring around the base with a lot of bolt holes, the two hulls were positioned and the poles were attached as cross members. It looked like a giant Hobie Cat. The forward cross member served as a mount for the mast step and the aft one for the outboard motor.

Well, this is how Bill and Kelly were able to turn their project into reality. Vince did the welding for them and purchased all the aluminum light poles and enough aluminum angle and channel to supply deck stringers and framing for a nice streamlined cabin with 5'8" headroom, large plexiglass ports, and two hatches to let in a little island breeze. The carpenters did a great job working mostly on weekends. They found a used aluminum mast, sails, and rigging from a storm damaged sloop which fit perfectly. While Bill advanced his woodworking skills, Kelly became quite a seamstress, sewing all the curtains, sail covers, and cushions. The most expensive item on board the Papcat was the brand new 30 HP Johnson outboard.

I helped them find some of the hardware, tanks, sinks, stove, and a trampoline net. With a few days off for fishing and diving, the heart was beating in Papcat's little keels in less than a year.

The total cost, give or take a couple of hundred bucks, was $21,000. They've added a lot more since they went for their maiden voyage: navigational electronics, stereo, and wind generator, but that's not bad to get riding on the wind in a catamaran on a tight budget. This is the way to do it, American ingenuity... The achievable dream. And here we were sailing aboard it. You might not be a millionaire but you can live like one. At age 55 Bill says he's got it all now, a wooden sailboat and a Harley. Kelly says she's never bored because today is not a rehearsal for tomorrow.

The last time I saw Bill and Kelly they were in Saint Kits. The boat was holding up well. They had a new 30 HP Honda to replace the old Johnson. We dove up some lobsters and cooked them on the grill and they showed me the bronze ship builder's plate they had made, giving me credit as design producer and name sake for the Papcat. So if you see her sailing around, give them a hail. I'm sure they're good for a cocktail at sundown.

EGYPTIAN CHARTER

I've received a couple of letters this year asking about adapting boats for foreign guests. In one case a fellow cruiser's in-laws were coming from Sweden for an extended cruise. Another captain was selling his boat to an Italian family who wanted to go out on the boat for a week before they bought it. Both groups spoke very little English and neither had much sailing experience. I replied with stories about several foreign charters and some of the ideas we had used to make the guests more comfortable. In both cases they responded that they had good results, although the Italian group had some rainy weather.

My most successful group was from Egypt. They spoke no English and wanted to bring sheep on board the 110 foot power boat they'd chartered for two weeks, but instead were given a refund of their $25,000. I watched all this from a 68 foot ketch/motor sailor I was taking care of for a broker in Venezuela. His rate was only $6,000 a week so the difference gave me a lot of expense money to work with. I hired a college girl as an interpreter and we met with the charterers and solved the problem about the lamb meat. I installed an extra, small 110 volt freezer behind the wheel house. It seemed that the meat had to be butchered in a special way. My interpreter and I went shopping. We bought Arab music, books, magazines and four oriental rugs at Pier 1 Import store. We made sure my short wave radio would pick up news from Egypt and luckily the boat had a full set of awnings. They were light tan canvas and we usually left them at the dock, but on this charter they were quite appropriate. When the party boarded on the day of departure, I must say we were quite proud: the awnings were up, the carpets were laid out on the deck and Arab music was playing on the stereo. I thought the guests were going to hug me.

Another thing about foreign charterers: you must know their religious customs. The Muslims pray three times a day and I would stop the boat at the proper time and head her to the East. I had to learn what I could say to the women and what men do in the presence of the women. Putting up that full set of awnings whenever we anchored or were at the dock was a big pain in the stern, but surprisingly, the ladies helped us every time. Can you see me telling a fancy power boat captain on a $25,000 charter that I had women charter guests helping us put up the awnings?

You also have to learn what is taboo. These guests ate with their hands and my interpreter explained that if I was asked to eat with them I must not use a certain hand. On the third night, they asked Natalie, my cook, and me to join them for rice, dates and lamb. I forgot to tell Natalie and she ate with the wrong hand. It created quite a stir. The interpreter explained and eventually all was forgiven.

We planned an easy trip to Bimini and Nassau so the men could gamble. They also listened to the news each night, gathering around the short wave radio on deck, with great pleasure. When we got to Nassau we had two limousines waiting at the dock which took the group to the casino. They wanted me to wear one of their desert robes, which they wore during the whole trip, but I refused politely, even though they seemed remarkably cool in the heat. I didn't want to run into one of my Georgia hunting buddies at the casino wearing one of those get-ups. I was doing pretty well at the roulette table when our interpreter informed me not to do better than our guests or it would nix our chances for a tip. That took a bit more effort, but came out well and we made friends for life.

Another thing about foreign charters: you've got to be careful about bugs. Some people have never seen a big Bahama flying cockroach, and some, when bitten by a mosquito will swell up like a baseball. I used my old trick with 12 volt fans when the breeze was not enough under what the guests called "de tent."

The last important tip is to plan ahead on your paper work. Make sure you have visas for the U.S., Bahamas, etc., in case your guests want to fly out of a different port, or you break down or the weather interrupts your schedule. I find having foreign guests always offers a challenge and definitely broadens ones horizons.

Since then, I have taken two of their cousins out, one time in Saint Thomas and another in Martinique. I had Natalie, the cook from Malta, with me on all these trips and the last trip they gave her a golden Rolex as a tip. One of the biggest laughs we had on the trip was when they asked me about nicknames and I said sometimes people call me a boat jockey. They said that's a coincidence because we made some good friends ashore in Martinique that called us camel jockeys. We all had a big laugh.

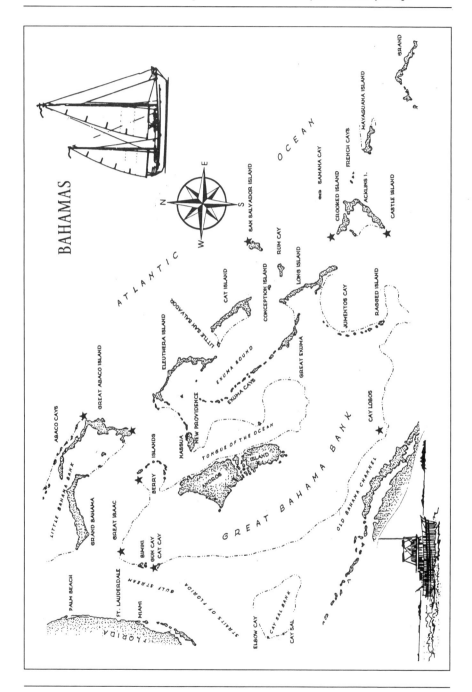

7 DAYS IN THE BAHAMAS

She is a 46 foot ketch, narrow in the beam, tall rigged, nice deep midship cockpit, and plenty of room down below. This is what I was looking forward to. On the down side she is short on water and freezer space for a charter boat and draws 6 ft. 4 inches. You really have to play the tides without hampering the charter's schedule too much. But when you are skippering for a charter boat company you can't complain too much about the boat or you won't get any work with them anymore.

I had my own charter boat for 10 years so I am set in my ways. I bring my own tools, water pump for the engine, diving and fishing gear, flag charts, G.P.S., tapes. On this trip I will be bringing a big cooler and 3 five gallon jugs of water. I can hear the charter boat company workers saying now, do you believe the stuff this guy brings? Some even feel sorry for me and help me load up.

Seven days to the Bahamas with 3 couples in their thirties, two businessmen, an engineer, 2 housewives and a nurse. The form says "no sailing experience". Sometimes that's good, you can count on what they are going to do, nothing you haven't showed them yet.

Well by this time it's 10 a.m. and they arrive in two rental cars. One with the people, and one with all the food and the gear. They seem nice midwesterners. A little nervous, maybe. We are sizing each other up. They are looking at my make-shift hat band, beard and rigging knife. I am watching the way they move to assist me in making assignments for duties aboard the boat. They asked me what I think of them so far. I tell them to go unpack those "hard suit cases" on the boat and then take them up and leave them at the charter boat company office. I give them a book I do on the Florida Keys that has a suggested provisionings list in it, checking it against what they bought. That seems to calm them down some.

I show them how to operate the heads and assign the sleeping arrangements so everyone will know where to store their gear. By noon we are going out of the inlet. It's blowing 15 knots from the N.E. and a good swell running. We are making about 6.5 knots under full sail. By and by two of the guys and one of the girls aren't feeling so good. So we decide to sail down to Miami, anchor, and cross the gulf stream tomorrow at daylight. Dan the engineer puts my 2 trolling rods out and about half way to Miami we pick up two nice dolphins.

I put one of the girls on the wheel and go aft to skin the fish. One of the reasons I really like this job, eating fresh fish, sailing, diving, and seeing these people have the time of their lives. I got one of the women and slipped down into the galley and fried up some of the Dolphin in butter, lime juice and soy sauce. The fish smells so good cooking, everybody comes alive. One of the guys says, "I never thought that smell of cooking fish would make me feel better".

Sailing in to Key Biscayne anchorage with a beautiful sunset full in our face, we drop the hook, have some drinks, more fish and talk about tomorrow's trip. I really enjoy a first time charterer's enthusiasm about the waters, the fish and the adventure itself. I tell them you can lay home on the couch and watch it on National Geographic or you can get out here and do it, but you can't do both.

5:30 a.m. we are up and out, breakfast under way. The wind is about the same as it was the day before. Under full sail the breaking sun reflects the spray of the gulf stream, coming occasionally over the windward rail.

"OK folks," says I, "don't want no pukers or burners to-day, let's get that number 15 on and those patches behind your ears (a new seasick medicin)". Why hell, I am no doctor but I think it's part of my job to know the sun-and the weather. I find that by and by in that hot Bahama sun, the charterers get headaches at night if they don't wear hats and sunglasses to protect them from the heat and the glare.

We are steering 130° for the Gun Key light. The wind has eased up a bit and we are out of the sight of land. A first time for everybody on board but me. We don't pick up the Gun Key light until about 5:30 p.m. I figure we can make it through the channel around the light before dark. We put up the yellow quarantine flag and I tell them it's tradition on sighting land, everybody should have a shot of rum. About 10 min. later we hook a nice bonito on the line. We don't get the fish in the boat, because the boys whack him with the gaff hook about twenty times and can't get him in. I yell from the wheel, "Hey, you guys ain't playing golf back there, you know!"

Centerfold makes it through the Gun Key Channel, we anchor and all go for a swim that refreshes everybody. Another beautiful sunset with the Gun Key Lighthouse silhouetted against it. The charterers break out the bar-b-que; it is going to be red meat tonight. After supper in the cockpit, another boat comes into the anchorage. The captain and crew row over for a couple of drinks and discuss the crossing. Everyone is in bed by 10:30 p.m.

The next morning at about eight, a squall comes through and washes the boat off nicely. I go on deck for a shower explaining to the charterers the shortage of fresh water in most of the Bahamas. After breakfast and a swim, we motor into Cat Cay to clear customs. It's about a two mile trip. Cat Cay is a beautiful little island owned by the Rockwell Corporation.' It's a private club, but they let you tie up there overnight to clear customs and get provisions. Everyone is amazed about how clear the water is, even in the harbor. Bill and his wife meet a couple who live on the island and they take the other charterers on an island tour aboard golf carts, the Cat Cay's main mode of transport.

We leave Cat Cay heading for the northern end of Gun Cay, where there is a beautiful little harbor with a nice beach and good snorkeling on the western side. We put the dinghy and motor in the water and make for the beach to snorkel. The girls want to look for shells. I like this idea because I am able to check out everyone's snorkeling ability on the beach in shallow water. They feel more secure in learning to breathe and adjusting their masks and snorkels. It takes about an hour for all to feel comfortable.

We swim over to the reef for some sightseeing.

This is another part of my job I really enjoy: watching these folks freak out when they see all the beautiful color of the fish and coral of the underwater world. You can almost feel the vibrations coming through the water.

We stay out on the reef for about an hour. Back at the boat they can't stop talking about all the different kinds of fish. We have a "fish i.d. book" aboard, so they try to pick out all the different types of fish they have seen.

Later on that night after supper we go to the beach and build a fire. Several of the couples disappear into the darkness, so I get a ride back to the boat.

The next morning, all the crew accounted for, we set sail for Bimini with a fine breeze; it is about ten miles to the North. The color of the water on the entrance into the Bimini Harbor is fantastic: all the blues and greens in contrast with the white sand. I have to slow down while they take pictures.

"I'd really like to know what the magic is in a Harley Davidson motorcycle."

We tie up at Weeches dock and I introduce them to Jerry Francis the dock master. We have a few rums, lots of laughter and then take a walk down North Bimini's King's Highway past Maria the Hat Lady stand and three or four places where you can buy straw goods. The charters all get hats and shell beads. Twelve Bahamians are whooping it up while playing a fantastic game of dominos nearby.

Further down the King's Highway on the left is the Compleat Angler Bar. There are a lot of pictures of fish and Ernest Hemingway on the inside walls. Good drinks and something called "the ring game" which consists of a brass ring attached to string hung from the ceiling being swung toward a hook stuck into the tavern's wall. The owner of the bar, Ossie Brown, comes over and gives some lessons.

It is time to go back to the boat. Jerry, the dock master, is there with his guitar and we all sit around and sing while the girls fix supper. Jerry stays, of course, and after dinner he makes up several songs about my charterers. I give him clues as to their jobs and hints about their personalities. It is great, Jerry's a true on-the-spot poet. The party goes on into the wee hours.

The next morning, it is out to Turtle Rocks, to snorkel getting fish and conch. It is only about three miles south of the harbor so we don't put up the sails. Turtle Rocks is one of my favorite dive spots. There is an easy place to anchor over coral ledges in about ten feet of water. This is great for the charterers; they don't have to swim any distance to see all the great things underwater and they have the boat directly overhead for security. Later in the afternoon we drift out on the Bahama Banks and pick up fifteen nice conch.

By this time, everyone is exhausted, so we motor back to Bimini, tie up and feast on scorched conch and a thick conch chowder over rice. We're asleep by nine dreaming of tomorrow's sailing and fishing.

We get some rigged ballyhoo the next morning from Bob's Bait and Tackle heading out for some serious trawling under sail. The winds are perfect. By four that afternoon we have picked up two barracuda and two large dolphin. Back in Bimini that night we give a fellow on the dock named Beau the barracuda in exchange for skinning and filleting the dolphin. The charterers go down to the Compleat Angler after supper where the band is playing for a dance.

The next morning, the charterers want to dive on the shipwreck called the Sapona, it is an old wrecked concrete ship about halfway between Bimini and Gun Cay. She is two hundred feet long and is laying in fifteen feet of water with most of her super structure exposed. She is famous for being the bombing target that squadron of planes that were lost and blamed on the Bermuda Triangle decades ago. My companions get into exploring the Sapona, amazed at the things to do around Cat Cay, Bimini Island Chain.

The last night ashore, we meet Bonefish Tommy. We decide to go fishing with him the next morning before we sail back to the states, Tommy has a sixteen foot skiff and he takes the group out among the flats of Bimini, to try for one of the hardest fighting fish around. They get back the next morning around eleven with two bonefish and a permit. These guys can't say enough about Bonefish Tommy and the fishing action.

It is time to split and head back to Florida. We make a turn past the marina and wave good-bye to Maria the Hat Lady, Jerry, Bonefish Tommy and Beau the Barracuda Man. Another of the rewards of being a charter captain; my clients get to meet the people of the islands and see what they are like, the way they talk, sample their food and their Island Calypso music.

The charterers say they like the experiences with people as much as seeing the underwater world for the first time. A feeling of pride wells up inside me, another perk besides my job's pay. They will be back to visit their island friends and see the clear water and white sands of the Bahamas again.

Cat Island Bahamas, 1980. Cleaning conch with a wild group from Orangeburge, SC. The sisters, Don and a girl called "The Bull" who only ate Butterfinger candy bars.

FOUL WEATHER GEAR

━•━ ☰◈☰ ━•━

Here are some ideas I past on to some other young ship mates starting off in the buckeneer game (what we call the charter sailboat business). My crew would see me heading down the hatch and say, "Where are you going Captain?"

"Going down below to put on my rain gear so I look like the advertisement on a clam can and to see if I can make that big squall miss us." As fate would have it, usually, if you prepare yourself and put on all your rain gear, the squall will avoid you. If you don't it will hit you, and all your crew will be scrambling to put on their foul weather gear, leaving no one to run the boat. My wife calls it "rain gear." She says there is nothing foul connected with boating except a plugged up head. (I say a line fowled around your prop is a close second.)

Here is what we have come up with which has been passed on to and adopted by many salty souls: I use a Helly Hansen light rubber yellow jacket, priced at about $40, and cut longer than other brands. I take my hooded jacket to the canvas shop or sail maker and get them to sew a couple of soft clear plastic windows in each side of the hood, so when I turn my head, I can see.

I was lying on the aft deck steering with an emergency tiller one time, when one of my crew pointed over the stern at something. I turned my head to see what it was, and the hood got in my line of vision so I couldn't see what he was pointing at. A large wave almost washed me overboard. So, that's when I came up with the little window idea. Also, I ask the sail maker to sew a clear plastic piece over my left wrist so I can see my watch without pulling up the sleeve.

For rain pants we use the light rubber ones with a drawstring (or elastic) which only come up to the waist and with legs baggy enough to get over your boots or shoes so if you have to go to the head, you don't have the problem associated with the bib type. For those who sail in cold weather (God help you), just wear a pair of sweat pants and a sweat shirt under this rig.

I use orange pants so that I can be identified as the "captain." This I learned from an old friend, Sam Gerring, on the brig Unicorn. He had the combination yellow coat and orange pants and all the crew wore yellow with big numbers in glow tape on the back and smaller numbers on the front. I adapted that when racing at night. "Hey number five, slack the main halyard!" It's mighty handy to yell a number over the roar of the wind. Especially with a large crew when you are not able to see a face.

Everyone on board wears a belt on the outside of their rain coat with a large sheath or rigging knife on it. Call me old fashioned, but a sailor without a knife is like a shark without teeth. In my right pocket I carry one of those flat disposable flashlights and my sailing gloves. In my left pocket I carry a police whistle so someone can hear me if I fall overboard.

For sea boots we use the old topsiders, black with a white sole or Douglas Gill blue tops with glow tape along the sides. Every 6 months or so we give them a coat of Armorall, it seems to make them last longer. When it's blowing and the rain is really coming down hard, I have a pair of old aviator goggles with a coat of Rain-Ex on the lenses. This allows me to look into the eye of the rain or look straight up into the rigging. For long stints at the wheel we use the black rubber fisherman's gloves with an inexpensive cotton glove underneath. This keeps the water out and gives a little extra insulation.

Now, for the last couple of years we have made some long deliveries. Luckily, the vessels were equipped with weather FAX aboard. We were able to avoid heavy weather and use the wind to our advantage. So, instead of "There we were on the bowsprit trying to get the jib down" I guess the stories we will be telling our grandchildren now will be: "There I was at the navigation station running out of FAX paper with only four megatypes of ram and a glitch in my floppy disk."

A SPEACH AND SLIDE SHOW IN BALTIMORE

Here is an idea of what its like on the speakers circuit. Last spring I flew north to do a seminar on the Florida Keys as a guest of the Chesapeake Windjammers Association. I hadn't been to Baltimore in about 10 years.

I had just left a charter of spring break women from Wake Forest University who partied and played rock and roll music constantly. The next night I was dining at the engineer's club with past and present commodores and a musician playing the harp. What a contrast.

The dinner was held in a beautifully restored old mansion. We walked from there to the historical society building, where my talk would take place, along a street lined with traditional ironwork balconies. Truly, charm and culture are not dead.

What a great bunch of sailing enthusiasts. Their excellent visual equipment staff provided a theater-sized screen for my slides and a laser pointer. There was lots of laughter and an excellent intermission which I spent drinking punch and autographing books. As they say down South, a good time was had by all of the 200 or so members.

I stayed an extra day to tour the Baltimore harbor as recommended by Commodore Stamps. The downtown area has been restored beautifully with its harbor walk featuring the Pride of Baltimore II, a graceful replica of an old Chesapeake sailing vessel. The captain had just given a talk for the Windjammers, so I used that as a calling card along with my press pass to get on board for a personal tour and some excellent refreshments.

The Pride of Baltimore is a fine traditional sailing ship and she is well maintained by her crew of enthusiastic young mariners.

It was a beautiful sunny day, and there were street performers and various kinds of entertainment all around the harbor walk as well as the usual shops and restaurants with food of every kind imaginable. With a harbor like this to sail in and out of, I can see where the previous night's audience gets its enthusiasm for the maritime life.

Inner city marinas give me a concern for security, so I did a little survey, asking 10 or 15 people if they had ever had a problem with safety or theft. Everyone spoke in positive terms. The Harbor View Marina has plenty of transient slips and stands by on channel 16 VHF 24 hours a day. The dockage rates are comparatively reasonable at $1.35 per foot. Amenities include floating docks, a floating island pool, and a neat bar called The Afterdeck. After a couple of grogs there, we went to the marina restaurant called Pier 500. The service was great, and we stuffed ourselves on crabs and fish.

From there we took the water taxi for a tour of the harbor at night a spectacular ride. The manager of the marina's health club happened to be on board and invited me for a workout in the morning to get back in shape.

I couldn't make it because my flight to the Keys was too early, but I did get a chance to check out the Inner Harbor East Marina. Its rates are only $1.05 per foot for floating docks, and it is open from 8 a.m. to 8 p.m.

Then there is the Baltimore Marine Center at Lighthouse Point. Its rates are $1.25 per foot, and it has a 55-ton travel lift for haulouts and any repairs you might need. A mechanic is on duty seven days a week.

All in all, Baltimore is a real trip. There is also the National

Aquarium, the Concert Pavilion, the Science Center, the Baltimore World Trade Center, and the Maritime Museum. Camden Yards baseball park and Fort McHenry National Monument are also a short ride away.

Baltimore Harbor sure has changed since my last visit. I guess we will have to alternate between Annapolis and Baltimore on our next trip through the Chesapeake.

DAVY JONES' LOCKER

Davy Jones' Locker is a term used to describe the place of burial at sea. As a charter boat captain I get a number of requests to marry people on board and to take ashes of the deceased offshore, perform a little ceremony, and sprinkle the deceased's remains over the side.

Over the last couple of years we've had several calls asking for advice on how to do burials at sea, which is not the most cheerful subject, but interesting. It's a last request of many a famous sailor. My wife and I have done about a dozen or so funerals at sea from our charter boat, each of them definitely an adventure.

First we have to check the legality of putting anything in a particular body of water. Lakes, rivers, and oceans all have different rules. Ashes are okay for the Atlantic Ocean, but flowers, wreaths, or banners must be made of a special biodegradable material. We must also use a special biodegradable bag for the ashes.

Our first experience with a burial at sea came from a previous charterer who was in the funeral business. It was quite an elaborate ceremony. The woman who had died owned a house on the water, so we took our sailboat to her dock. A tent was set up on the lawn. Before we left we ate a very nice lunch and listened to a three-piece band. Then we took 11 people out into the Gulf Stream.

Going down the canals on the way out we got a lot of strange looks from people on their docks who were staring at all the men and women in their black suits and dresses.

I went about 4 miles offshore where I read a special section from the Bible. We sang several spirituals, and I fired my .38 pistol into the air three times.

Another captain had warned me to start the ashes going and dump the bag so it doesn't blow everywhere, but it was a beautiful flat, calm day and I was caught up in the reverence of the ceremony. I started the ashes and poof! They went all over everyone, on the bimini top, everywhere. Two of the ladies broke out laughing and said that was just like her, even her last moment could not be contained. That broke the tension, thank goodness. Then, like magic the wind picked up and we had a very nice sail back to the yacht club where we tied up, went to the bar and drank a toast to the deceased .

I heard later on that the group partied late into the night. It was said to be like an old-time Irish wake.

Our next experience was a group from Miami Beach. There were 21 guests in all, so I had to charter a bigger boat for this one. It was not through a funeral home, so I asked the guests if there were any special requests for the deceased. They referred me to his brother. My questions were, "Was he a sailor?" "Did he have a love for the ocean?" I also asked what section of the Bible to read from. The brother replied, "No, the sailboat was my idea. I have never been on one before. As for my brother, he said his wife is such a klutz that she would surely knock over the urn containing his ashes if it was left around the house, and he would end up in the vacuum cleaner. That's why he wanted his ashes sprinkled at sea."

I have learned to try to schedule burials at sea in good

weather. We make the boat trip as short as possible, and ask the charterers to wear soft-soled shoes. If you have two or more speakers for the deceased, have them agree in advance who will speak first to eliminate any argument at sea. One time we had a Catholic priest and a Baptist minister who argued for about half an hour while we floated around waiting in uncomfortable silence. I won't go into details, but I'm sure you get my drift. We try to have music or singing on board, and divide it so there is some when we leave and some when we return.

In all our experience, a funeral at sea starts out to be quite a somber affair, but when you return to shore there seems to be an exhalted feeling of fulfillment and release. After all, they say we come from the sea, and to the sea we shall return.

STEADY BINOCULARS

I have had a pair of 7x50 rubber-coated binoculars since about 1972. They are pretty beat up but they work well. I tried some 10x50s, which were more powerful and provided a better image, but I could not hold them still enough to keep the vibration from blurring the image. At the Fort Lauderdale Boat Show I was talking to my friend Milt Baker from Blue Water Books and Charts about getting a pair of Steiner binoculars with the built-in compass bearing and a range finder. He said I should stop by his store and try the new Canon 12x36 I S binoculars. They have a stabilizer which eliminates almost all vibration. He said it was developed for use in video cameras. I tried them out and they work well.

On a boat it is very important to be able to identify things at long distances like birds working over fish, spotting a landmark to identify a particular island, reading the number on a marker, or the name of a vessel so you can call it on the radio. My charterers really enjoy using the binoculars at night to look at the stars. Being a charter boat captain, I get on a lot of boats I am not familiar with so I use my binoculars to check the rigging and the condition of any equipment on the masthead. It's really handy and it saves you a ride in the Boson's chair. A couple of times I have spotted a worn out sheave and internal halyard block that warned me to be careful when raising that sail. Nothing is worse than getting a halyard jammed between the sheave and the cheek of the block.

Don't get me wrong. A thorough inspection of the rigging is better than a quick check with the binoculars, but when you are leaving in about an hour it's a handy little trick to know.

MAGICA

Here is a product that has saved me a couple of times. The first incident was when I was running a racing sailboat for a friend of Jimmy Buffet's. We were in a series of races off of Ft. Lauderdale, and I really wanted to make a good impression. The owner said he wouldn't be on board for the next two races, so I figured I could relax a little bit that night.

There was a party aboard Ondine with fancy drinks called rusty nails which were flowing like water. I got stuck in a corner talking to some of the crew and the only hors d'oeuvres I could reach were the Doritos and bean dip. I hadn't had any supper, so what, with telling stories and drinking and eating that dip the next thing I knew I was blitzed. I barely made it back to the boat.

The next day I woke up late with the worst hangover I ever had. On top of that the owner had changed his mind and was back on board for the next two races.

It was blowing 30 knots. Wouldn't you know that's just the weather this boat was made for? We had a chance to take an easy first or second in the race.

Going around the third mark I had to go forward and help my crew with the heavy spinnaker and man, did I feel sick. If I threw up then, the sight of his captain getting seasick wouldn't have made a good impression on the owner. So I let it go in a full sailbag on deck. In all the confusion, nobody even noticed.

We took a second in the race, and with all the excitement when we got back to the dock I forgot to take the sail out of the bag and wash it off.

The next race we set the big starcut chute and it had a brown stain on it which looked like a Rorschach print. The owner said there must be something rusty in that sail locker staining our sails. "Yeah, a rusty nail," says I under my breath. I told him I would take care of it as soon as we got back. The next day I took a spray bottle of Magica, put it on the sail and it cleaned it perfectly. (We went on to take first in class and fourth overall.)

The next time Magica came to my rescue was when I bought a little 24-foot wooden sloop, a real classic, for only $2,000. I figured I could clean her up and turn her around for an easy $5,000, but I hadn't checked the sails closely enough. They were in good shape but they had terrible rust stains on them. I used Magica again and the stains came out like a dream. I also soaked the sails for about four hours then spread them out on the lawn to dry. They appeared to be good as new.

I later found out that I knew the holder of the patent of the Magica formula, Captain Williams of the Fox River Marina. He acquired it from a Danish man the captain and his wife met and befriended back in the '70s. Captain Williams' son-in-law, Bob Everhart, has refined the product into different sized tubes, bottles, and sprayers. It has no harsh chemicals, yet it will clean stainless steel, fiberglass, plastic, and it even got a stain off one of my wife's beautiful blouses. I hope you find this helpful.

"One advantage of being at sea all your life, you'll never be in an earthquake."

The family.

Playing the drums with the late Ozzie Brown.

LOG OF NAUTICA ON THE WEST COAST OF FLORIDA

━━◆━━

The mate was down below making a last minute check on the provisions as I turned the Nautica gently to port into Flamingo Harbor on the edge of the Everglades. We were to pick up our charter here ~ Mr. and Mrs. Parker and family. We would cruise north out into the Gulf of Mexico and along Florida's west coast. The end of March was a good time of the year to do this trip ~ not too hot, not too cold and generally an east-southeast prevailing wind. We had just gotten the vessel secured when we saw the Parkers, their son and daughter, walking down the dock.

We piped them aboard and the mate grabbed his guitar and gave them a few versus of the "Sloop John B." Then there were the introductions, "Welcome aboard the Nautica, I am Frank Papy your captain, licensed by the U.S. Coast Guard and Panama, and this is the first mate Bill Behze. Bill has 15 years sailing experience and is a helluva chef. Please don't call him a cook." "Mr. Mate. will you please help the Parkers stow their gear and Mr. Parker, I will give you a tour of the vessel. She is a 3 years young Morgan OI 41 ketch. She has a diesel engine, 4 headsails, a main and mizzen…"

As 8 bells struck (4 pm), the mate had finished helping the Parker's stow their gear and took them ashore to the state operated wildlife museum. I grabbed 2-6 packs of beer and went over to the fuel dock to bargain for some fresh caught Red fish. Eventually everyone was back aboard and cocktails were served ~ rum for the mate and myself and white wine for the Parker's. The mate outdid himself as usual this evening cooking up pan-fried Red fish, cornbread with melted cheese and a big green salad.

The next morning after breakfast, we got a couple of extra blocks of ice and were on our way out of Flamingo, with a SW wind at about 14 knots. As we sailed toward Cape Sabel the mate shouted, "Wow, look what's behind us." It was an old bugeye ketch under full sail ~ what a sight. Everyone onboard got their cameras and started clicking. We reached along side by side for about an hour. Soon we had rounded Cape Sabel and as we headed for the beach for lunch we watched the bugeye disappear to the north.

At about 1 pm we dropped the sails and anchored for lunch off one of the most beautiful white sandy beaches you'll ever see anywhere. The mate cooked up a spinach salad and some crab bisque. Later he took the Parker's ashore in the dinghy for some shelling and a swim. After lunch, we picked up the hook and headed north into the Little Shark River basin, a well protected harbor. There were several boats in the harbor including the big bugeye ketch we had sailed with earlier in the day. They hailed us as we entered the harbor and invited us to raft up. Mr. Parker gave his OK, and soon with fenders out and extra springlines secured, we were rafted up with the "Blue Seas." The mate then preceded to plan supper with the wife of the captain of the bugeye, while I did some work on the fresh water pump.

Dinner was soon served aboard the "Blue Seas" ~ wine and spaghetti with white clam sauce for 12 people who had met only hours before who were now laughing and joking like life long friends. It must be the sea air, the wine or a combination of the two ~ a very relaxing evening.

It had been a late night, and I was the first one up the next morning. I put the water on to boil, sliced up some oranges, put a big pan of bacon on the stove and did my old trick of waking people up by their noses ~ sprinkling some fresh ground coffee on the hot stove. Within 16 minutes everyone was up ~ "What's that smell?"

Up on deck Mr. Parker had his binoculars out watching the tremendous variety of birds in the mangroves and trees nearby. The crew of the bugeye were bottom fishing ~ catching some small snappers and grunts. Christine, the Parker's daughter was being pulled up the mast of the bugeye in a boson's chair for some aerial shots. It was a very nice day ~ clear with an easterly wind about 12 knots. After breakfast we said good bye to our friends on the "Blue Seas," set the genoa and main to head around Cape Romano shoals.

As we sailed along, Mr. Parker asked if the family could participate more in the sailing. We wanted them to learn as much about sailing and sea life as was possible on this trip. I agreed. We figured we would head up to Naples sail all night and get to Ft. Myers Beach about 4 am. The mate set up a watch schedule for the Parkers.

When we anticipate an all night sail, we give the charterers a big lunch during the day and then Bill makes an evening meal in his big black iron pot, which sits on the stove all night long. This time he cooked up some ham, peas, rice and onions in a delightful mixture. This arrangement allows the watches to eat anytime they want without disturbing anyone else resting below. After another beautiful sunset, especially beautiful under sail, I went below for a couple hours sleep, as the mate and Mr. Parker's daughter stood watch.

At 9:30 when I relieved the mate, the wind was freshening, so we dropped the genoa and bent on the working jib. It cut our speed in half, but made for a more comfortable sail. I put Mr. Parker's son on the helm and had myself a steaming plate of rice and ham and a mug of coffee. The stars were out in full force and other than being a little on the chilly side, it was a beautiful night for sailing. Mr. and Mrs. Parker came on deck about 1 am to enjoy the night sailing. I made them put on safety harnesses over their foul weather gear since they wanted to go up on the foredeck.

The mate came up on deck around 2 am with the loom of Ft. Myers Beach in sight. I stayed up another couple of hours and at about 4:30 am I helped the mate drop the sails and anchor. We put out two anchors for good measure and then turned in for a well deserved rest.

The mate and I were up at about 10:30. And as the Parker's slept we upped anchor and motored into Pine Island Sound behind the beautiful beaches of Sanibel and Captiva Islands. We could have sailed, but the batteries needed charging and the mate wanted to get brunch ready for our charterers. As we motored through the Sound with the Parkers eating brunch in the cockpit, the mate shouted "porpoises on the bow." There were about a dozen of them playing around the boat for about 10 minutes. Everyone forgot about brunch, went for their cameras and took pictures.

Further up the Sound, we soon arrived at the South Seas Plantation Marina, one of my favorites, and a place I thought the Parkers would really like. It's a fancy marina at the north end of Captiva Island with all kinds of facilities and great beaches for swimming and shelling nearby. Once docked, Mrs. Parker and her daughter went shelling and to my surprise Mr. Parker and his son volunteered to help the mate and myself scrub down the Nautica. With a little Jimmy Buffet music and all the extra help, we seemed to get the job done in no time at all. And to top it all off, the ladies were soon back from the beach and fixed us all a great lunch. That afternoon, the Parkers went ashore and I took a nap in my hammock on deck. That night we all went out for supper at the marina restaurant. Mr. Parker announced that the next day he would be playing golf with some people he had met during the day and that the ladies would spend the day at the beach.

The mate and I always look kindly on a lay day and while the Parkers were off doing their thing, we found our own things to do ~ like helping a novice racer tune his rigging. The reward for offering this kindly hand was five pounds of fresh gulf shrimp.

The Parkers were soon back aboard with five guests from the beach and golf course. I made some of the guests take off their hard shoes. A couple of them seemed a little disturbed at first, but got over it. We had cocktails, shrimp with dip and Bill and I entertained them with guitar, conga drums and rhythm instruments for everyone else moraccas, sticks, etc. Then out to dinner again. A table for 12 with Mr. Parker at the head of the table. Many toasts were made to the beautiful islands, the Nautica and her crew.

The next day was clear, with the wind very light out of the southeast. Everyone was up by nine ~ some a little under the weather. So we decided to take it easy and motor up to Cabbage Key, a beautiful little island with no access by land. There is a small bar and restaurant there and a lot of history. The big building was once the home of Mary Rinehart, a famous writer of mystery novels. Another interesting place to visit in the area is Usppa Island, also not accessible by land. It has 20 private homes and a club. In order to go ashore, you must be a member or make arrangements through the South Seas Plantation. After touring around Cabbage Key, it was 2:30, the wind was picking up out of the northeast, so we decided to sail up into Charlotte Harbor ~ again porpoises on the bow. We had the main and genoa up and the Nautica was cutting along nicely. Around 5:30 we dropped sail and anchored off Cape Hase ~ 12 miles up Charlotte Harbor. Another super sunset, as the mate rigged up the bar-b-que grill on the stern.

Our meal for the evening was lamb shish kabob and rice. Mr. Parker broke out two nice bottles of wine and we all settled down for another of the mate's feasts. It was a quiet night with a lot of stars until 3:00 am when a couple of heavy rain squalls came through. The mate and I put out a second anchor and kept watch until dawn.

Mr. Parker's family had some kind of connection with the circus industry and he mentioned the day before that he wanted to get into Sarasota to see some friends and for the kids to get to a couple of famous museums in the Sarasota area. So at about 6 am we got both anchors up and shoved off for Sarasota with the winds out of the east at 18 to 20 knots. Running out of Boca Grande Channel with main and working jib, we saw the Gulf had quite a chop so we ran as close to shore as possible keeping out of the heavy swells. Lunch that day was stuffed peppers and rolaids. At about 1 pm we left the Gulf through New Pass and headed for Marina Jacks right in downtown Sarasota. The Parkers were soon off to see the sights and we didn't see them again until the next morning.

After breakfast at the marina restaurant, we headed for our last destination, Passe Grille Channel just north of Tampa Bay. With clear skies, we shoved off about 10:30 with the wind out of the southeast at 8 knots. This was the last day of the trip and since we had the right wind, the mate and I figured we'd give the Parkers a real thrill and break out the spinnaker. It's an old used sail, too big for the boat, but you'd never know it to look at it. It's red with a black and white maltese cross in the center. She really had us going along nicely. Everyone was impressed and took some nice pictures. We made quite a sight passing Anna Maria Island, a famous fishing spot. A couple of small runabouts came by for a closer look.

The mate being the ham he is flagged one of them over, took Mr. Parker's camera, got into their boat and took some shots of the Nautica with the spinnaker flying. It was a little more difficult getting him back on board underway, but he made it OK with the camera intact. Soon after his boarding, I picked up the large pink hotel I use as a landmark to find the Passe Grille Channel. Taking the spinnaker down was a team effort and the Parkers really did help.

There was a small sailboat race going on right near the channel entrance so it was a duck and dodge experience on the way in. We were headed for the Terra Verde Marina on Terra Verde Island just south of St. Petersburg. As we approached the marina, we had a straight shot at the dock, so I stood alongside of Mr. Parker, directing him, and he brought her in just fine. We spread the spinnaker out on the lawn to dry and went for a farewell supper and many toasts to a great crewed yacht vacation on Florida's west coast.

The Parkers and I became great friends. My wife and I took them several times sailing in the Bahamas and I lined up a job for Mr. parker's daughter as a deckhand aboard a yacht sailing out of Côte d'Azur. She worked on the boat for almost two years. We still keep in touch with some of the family members.

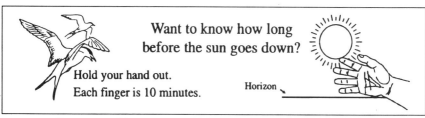

Want to know how long before the sun goes down?

Hold your hand out.
Each finger is 10 minutes.

Horizon

Here is an old trick to see how much day light you've got left.

Iwirn 52, 1979. The sand and sea with Jimmy Haft.

IF ONLY COLUMBUS KNEW

I would say the Columbus Day Regatta weekend rates along with the sailing family's summer vacation. I think I can make this statement because from Palm Beach to Marathon, Florida there are quite a few boats that the only time they go out is for the Columbus Day Regatta and the summer vacation cruise.

I have been sailing in the Columbus Day Regatta and social event since 1967. I have only been registered in the race five times. The other times I just sailed along and I haven't missed one of these unique events yet. Last year there were about 1100 boats registered and an estimated 4,500 vessels that came along for the fun and I mean fun! For those who don't know it's the weekend around the 12th of October. You leave Dinner Key marker on Saturday around 9 a.m. and sail down Biscayne Bay 20 miles to Elliott Key, anchor and sail back on Sunday.

There is every type of boat you can imagine. To accommodate these unusual boats the race community created categories like the gunkholing class and dowager class for boats thirty years and older. You can really see some strange rigs. Last year I saw a 55 foot cigarette type powerboat with a big A-frame mast that folded down on the bow when not in use-sailing along with a big spinnaker up. The amount of boats that gathered for this celebration last year was estimated at about 5,500, quite a sight to see on Biscayne Bay. You can forget about talking on the VHF radio, just listen and laugh at the antics.

One year, I heard a lady on a sailboat that was aground talking to the Coast Guard in distress. They asked how bad is she aground? "You know what is the trim of the vessel?" She replied, it's trimmed with teak.

Another time, the Coast Guard was asked to do a medical evacuation of a sick person with a helicopter from the boat. You know how the Coast Guard talk in that technical language, be advised that... etc.... etc. They asked the boat, what is the type of illness of this person? the captain of the boat replied, she has had too much to drink and she is up in the bow with a gun, going to shoot everybody, the pilot of the Coast Guard helicopter broke in on channel 16 and said, "I ain't taking that crazy woman on this helicopter.

Later on the same day, one boat called a friend and said he was sailing and had a problem. The spinnaker was caught in the mizzen mast on the boat sailing in front of him. Picture that in your mind. A big oil company used to bring a barge down with a big tent on it and a dance band. Anybody could take the dinghy over and join in the festivities. But times have changed. In the 1960's, a lot of the crews had t-shirts just alike. In the seventies, a lot of the crews wore nothing at all. What a show.

Watch out for the flying water balloons ~ anybody and everybody is vulnerable. After the race on Saturday, you anchor or raft up with some other sailors because you can't find your friends in the maze of boats and haze of some beers or rums or whatever. Watch the spinnaker riding, wind surfing, water skiing, ultra lights putting on a show... hot air balloons and a 35-foot Bill Healey boat that comes by with about 60 people on it.

The race has many famous participants. Famous boat builders and sailors like: Dave Westfall, Bill Souerell, Lee Creekmore and sailmakers like: Brad Mack on the Susanne, Charley Fowler, Marc Woods and Fred Bremmen. There are three big charter sailboats out of Miami that give up their trips to sail down with friends and party like: Bruce Purdy on the

Sea Explorer and Morning Star, and Steve Salum on the Sundance. They are quite a sight to see with 20 or 30 on board each one.

Six years ago it was a spinnaker start, I wasn't registered in the race but my boat just happened to be in the right spot at the right time and I was shown in the lead in a big color aerial photo on the front page of the paper, can you beat that?

Now when the sun goes down there is still more to see ~ boats show movies on their sails, weather permitting, and lots of music. Keep an eye on the weather. We break up the raft around midnight and anchor out of the way because usually around 3 a.m. a squall comes up and that's a show in itself. Boats dragging into one another, captains trying to break up a raft of boats with crews that have been drinking most all day is quite a job. But in my years of attending the race, I have never heard of any serious accidents.

Well, in the morning there is a group of small power boats that deliver the Sunday *Miami Herald*. They throw it in your cockpit as they come by (like the *Waterfront News*), so if you are sleeping out there, watch out that it doesn't hit you. The Sunday paper is heavy.

After a breakfast of an aspirin and Bloody Mary, you take your dinghy and look for some of your crew that's either passed out or become romantically involved.

The race back on Sunday usually has a later start to allow for these delays. The best place to observe the race on the final day is at the finish line, anchor off Key Biscayne for the grand finale, water balloons, mooning the race committee boat and topless girls who were too bashful to participate on the first day.

By 6:00 on the Sunday afternoon there are a lot of tired sunburned, happy sailors who will return the next year no matter what. I wonder what Columbus would say about all this done in his memory. Being a sailor himself, I think he would be proud.

Tips For The Race
1. Anchor in Biscayne Bay Friday night.
2. Take pre-cooked food.
3. Take warm clothes, last couple of years it's gotten chilly.
4. If you are meeting another boat, carry some very large, strange flag for identification.
5. If you don't have a boat, charter one for the race with a captain so you can party (it's about $300 per couple).

Holder "Nute" we would yell she's "headin" for the "alfalfa".

"With my writing I can make you feel, but the ultimate is to make you think."

"With my writing I can make you feel, but the ultimate is to make you think."

BOOT KEY HARBOR

I have sailed into many ports in my lifetime and it's rare to visit a place where you feel the people really belong there by their philosophy and appearance. All the people around Boot Key Marina (in the Florida Keys) look like John Huston, the movie producer, had picked them out to play the many characters who hung around the old fish house marina and shrimp docks.

In the late afternoon breeze about thirty times in the last ten years I have come drifting into the Boot Key Marina under sail on the sloop "Nautica. I drop the main and jib and coast up to the fuel dock. I tie up and step off and sit down under the great wooden roof built over the large dock that always had chairs and tables scattered about with maybe a half dozen folks sitting around having a cool one. My charter passengers would be straightening out on the deck and trying to figure out what is going on in this very laid back atmosphere. Then they come and join in the conversation and enjoy the breeze that blew under this big pavilion. Eventually the dock master comes along and gives me a slip assignment. Several times my charterers are so engrossed with the atmosphere and their new found friends l have to borrow a couple of the locals to help me move the boat over to my assigned berth. Everyone was always very helpful.

There were quite a few live-aboards who would say, "if you are going to B.B.Q. use my grill. It's much easier than digging yours out." "Just make sure that you clean it good when you finish." You would go to use it and it looked as if it hadn't been cleaned in months. So we used it and the charterers cleaned it well and the next day the guy would give us some fish. My charterers would say, "Why are you doing this?" And the old timers said, "Well hell!" "For cleaning my grill so nicely!!"

We would also walk over to the old fish house and get supper and a few beers. If we bought some fish the charterers usually haggled about the price over a dozen fish and when we got back to the boat we found out that he put 15 in the bag instead of a dozen. This was just an example of some of the ways they seemed to keep us entertained.

Sometimes they had dinghy races on Sundays up and down in front of the marina. Everybody who had a dinghy in the area seemed to show up. If it didn't have a sailing rig up they'd improvise one for the event. Usually there were fifteen or twenty entries. It was the most unorganized informal race I had ever seen. Most of the times the laughter and spontaneity lasted all afternoon, with the handicaps for each class for having too many beers or a nagging wife or being broke. After the races at supper time we boiled a lot of shrimp and spread some newspaper on the table and the charterers ate until they gagged.

There was an old fellow named "Al" who lived on a steel hull sloop who looked just like Gary Cooper. He usually won what was called the gaff rigged class. There were a couple of gals on a big motorsailor who always protested everything. There was an old Scotchman who was building a cement boat that calmed them down. I could go on for pages describing all the characters that lived at this marina.

Another interesting thing was a houseboat built on land with a neat little garden in front of it with a cannon and a sign that said, "A genuine authentic replica of a pirate cannon."

The scenery was so great around there. There were always watercolor artists hanging around making sketches of all the old trees, rustic buildings, and stacks and stacks of lobster traps. Ray Ellis, Millard Wells, and Cy DeCosse just to name a few. Well I guess they won't be hanging around there much more.

I just got back from a month in the Bahamas and in asking around about what's new in the Keys-on the count I do a cruising book on the Keys I have to keep posted on what's going on-a fellow sailor told me its the end of an era. They sold Boot Key, they tore the dock house down, and they charge $1.50 per foot to tie up there. That is like charging $200 a night for a motel room. They are going to knock the whole thing down and build a big condominium complex.

It seems that the more affluent we get the more sensitive we should be towards these places. I mean it's pretty obvious, writers write about them, artists paint them, and singers like Jimmy Buffet, Burdy Higgins, and Pineapple sing about them. I think the charm and rustic quaintness of the Keys needs preserving just like the reefs of John Pennecamp Park and the little Keys deer. But I guess that it is so intangible: this particular essence, and money is not. The next thing they'll do is sell the Key West sunset place.

Oh well, when you pull into a marina now nobody ever asks what type of folks live here. All they want to know is if there is Cable T.V., swimming pool, Jacuzzi, tennis courts, and a McDonalds nearby while the dock master, in his little white uniform and golf cart, screams at you over his bullhorn asking if you have American Express or VisaCard before he tells you if you can tie up or not.

Well I guess it's all been taken over by Lester Polyester and the Condo Cowboys. Like Gary Davis at Holiday Isle and Don Potter at Plantation Marina say, "That's progress." So, I will just have a rumrunner punch and think about it.

"Passion is at the heart of it and passion comes from the heart."

Upstairs bar at the Fero Blanco, Boot Key Harbor.

Gas dock, Marathon, Florida.

WORK A BOAT SHOW

My first boat show was in 1974. I write a cruising guide on the Florida Keys. When you walk into a boat show for the first time, the atmosphere on set up day is unbelievable. Everybody is rushing around with great anticipation in between lift-trucks, cranes and masses of giant wooden crates. You think to yourself, they will never have this ready in two days, but they always seem to get it done.

The second thing I learned was that you must rent everything; the ten by ten floor space, the carpet, curtains, chairs, signs, telephone, electricity, extra lights, even down to the ashtrays.

I was lucky with my first show. My booth was five spaces down from the bikini bathing suit dealer who had five models standing around looking beautiful. The folks that had the booth right next to them asked if I'd trade spots with them. They didn't want those girls distracting people from their product. Being a green horn at this business I agreed to change. Luckily, it worked out very well. Guys would come up in front of my booth, pretend to read it while looking next door at the ladies. Some of the males would be so engrossed I would say "That will be $9.95, please." They would just pay me without thinking and walk off. One gentleman even came back for another book and look.

All the different people you see and the styles of dress at the boat show is enough to entertain anyone. But don't let this fool you, you can't judge anyone by what they wear as to what they will spend. One night, there was a couple ~ she had a blue blazer and fancy boat shoes on and he was dressed the same, except for a $5,000 gold Rolex watch. Next to them was an old gent with khakis and work shoes on. I am talking to the couple and my wife is helping the old gentleman. The couple didn't buy anything. I talked to them for about twenty minutes. When I finished my wife said, "Can you get me two cases of books? This gentleman liked them and he is going to give them as Christmas gifts to one-hundred of his business customers." You never know.

After a hard night of working the show a lot of the exhibitors would gather at one of the bars and discuss all the funny things that happen so fast, during the show, you don't have time to talk about them, Man, I have heard some funny stories. At the height of the boat show a guy came in with a man behind him rolling a large old dirty engine on a hand truck. They went up to the exhibit that made the engines with all their fancy chrome motors cut in half and beautiful beige carpet and dumped the old motor right in the middle of the floor and started raising hell about his warranty, etc. I have never seen guys move so fast. They called him in the back, wrote him a check, cut out the carpet around the motor, drug it out of the way and within ten minutes, I would say, the guy was gone and they were putting a new piece of carpet in the spot. That's the way to get your warranty problems straightened out, I guess!

The paper that's used in the boat show in the brochures that are being passed out is unbelievable. One of the exhibitors said he ran through 6,000 leaflets in one night at the Miami boat show. Some people, I think, just try to see how many they can get.

The camaraderie that develops during the show amongst the exhibitors is fantastic. They develop a language all their own for types of spectators and nights of the show. For instance, Friday night is date night, all the young couples hand in hand.

Saturday night is the drinkers night, all the people who went out to supper and had three martinis then came out to the show. Sunday is family day. You have to watch out so the kids don't fall and hurt themselves or start up the engines on the boats.

All and all boat shows are OK. But there is a certain atmosphere I can't explain. Say, at an art show or exhibit somebody gets in free ~ either the exhibitor or the spectator ~ in other words, somebody is doing a benefit for the public in order to further the cause. Boat shows have become so expensive now. I hope they don't price themselves out of the market. You have to pay to park, it's $10 to $15 to get in and the prices at the food concession stands have gotten out of hand. A family of four who goes to the boat show on a Sunday and has a bite to eat can plan on spending $50 to $60. I think the idea of boat shows when they started was to promote new boaters and boating in general but it now is becoming a high priced hype! Last year there were three booths just selling guns and another booth selling see-in-the-dark scopes for $6,000 a piece, and something called the parabolic mike, so you can hear voices 100 yards away. I think some of this may scare off a young family thinking about getting into the leisure life of pleasure boating. They should appoint somebody to take a look at the overall picture rather than just filling up spaces and going for the almighty buck.

THE PORPOISE SHOW

One of my charters read this description in the log of the Nautica and said, "Frank, if you ever write a book, you should put this in it. All you have to do is close your eyes, read this and you are there."

We were anchored off Key Largo and my charters said they wanted to swim with the dolphins and these are some notes that they made for the log book to describe the show for my eight year old daughter.

Off the boat and on the shore for only a few hours, watching after the porpoise swam back into their individual pens, restlessly curling and blowing their tubes. I walked slowly away into the bright sunlight, my thoughts drifting through the palms, the smell of the wind out on the Gulf Stream, a strangely connected feeling. I immediately wanted to be back on the boat again, sailing fast, feeling the pull of the steering wheel in my palms, and watching the strain of the powerful headsails. I caught a glimpse of the lady trainer, lovingly squatting down, putting fresh fish in the bucket ready for the next show. Her skin was deep brown from the sun, and her blue eyes faded ashur pools, with two tiny black dots inward through her pupils, thoughtful waves of her lovers in their restricted, watery, salted cages. She swam out, floating the bucket of fish ahead of her artfully, to the center of the pool, to her small platform, as the new heads gathered for the second show, some blue, some bobbing, blowing a heavy Bud Beer breath, staling the morning breeze. They had paid their coins for the show. Their anticipation wanted it all. The dainty, brown skinned woman needed them to survive. I'm sure she made her excuse for knowing this, the dolphins didn't. Ever since God made them the most devout enchanted creatures of the sea. Her small brown toes on her dancing feet worked rapidly to keep her in time with the circling dolphins. Their powerful leaps and jumps dwarfing her tiny figure. It created a magnificent puzzle, why such powerful creatures would obey her every beckoned call. The individual introduction to each dolphin as he tail walked to his man given name. Children in the crowd comment to their parents, "Are these real Mom, or plastic with motors like you see at Disney World?" My attention is drawn to the swim suited patrons, who enter the pool of the dolphin's realm. The blue heads, and beer breaths are never there, only fresh, trusting young faces enter for the experience of a lifetime. The trainer emerges and strokes her favorite and whispers some unknown words into its unknown ear. Mystically the dolphins cast their spell on spectators and participants alike. A universal sweep, a temporary state of bliss, as their gentleness and power, used in ways not yet known to humans, as an example of peace and harmony on earth. How worldly, and happy they seem, to be able to pass this magical, complex knowledge on to us. But as seen in the eyes of our petite leader, the knowledge of the dolphins drip off of our participants, as they exit the pool, onto the dry, warm concrete, as if it was contained in the water itself, to evaporate into the breeze, and blow back out onto the Gulf Stream, in an unobserved, never ending circle.

"If you don't have a lot of siver and gold, have a lot of brass and love of life."

Canadian Charter's Michael and Barbara Web could not think of a name for their boat, so they named it "Papy".

IT'S NEVER TOO LATE

My last charter trip to the Berry Islands in the Bahamas was fantastic. We had two couples aboard and the charter company had hired a cook for the trip. We were about 6 days into the charter, anchored off a beautiful little beach. Annie, the cook, and I had taken the dinghy ashore and were cleaning some conch for hors d'oeuvres when we spied an elderly gentleman walking down the beach toward us. He watched us clean the conch for awhile, and I asked him if he was off the passenger ship that was anchored off shore and had brought some folks in for a B.B.Q. at another beach about a mile down the shoreline. "No", he replied, "that's my boat anchored over there." Annie chimed in, "I apologize for the Captain's comments, I think he said that because you have those Bermuda shorts on and the shirt to match. Don't mind him", she says, "he has been out at sea for six days."

I checked the boat out of the corner of my eye, she was a heavy offshore cruising double ender. He introduced himself, "I am Jan. I have seen you all around for the last couple of days, and it looks like you all could use a break." So, he invited us all over to his boat for cocktails. When Annie and I got back with the conch I informed our charters about Jan's invitation for cocktails. They said they would love to go and see his boat, so the six of us set off in a crowded dinghy for our visit. What hospitality. He had a 12 volt blender on board and made fresh rum mango daiquiris. Annie slipped back over to our boat and got the conch for hors d'oeuvres. Scorched conch and mango daiquiris, what a combination.

Jan gave us a tour of his boat and we settled in for a

beautiful sunset. I tactfully asked Jan how long he'd had the boat? He replied casually as if he could read our minds, "Ten years. I got it on my 78th birthday. Well it did not take a mathematical genius to figure out how old he was now. There was a long pause in the conversation. Annie broke the lull by paying Jan a compliment on what good shape he was in. Our charters invited Jan back to our boat for dinner.

After some delicious grilled wahoo and fresh ground coffee we settled back down in the cockpit under the Bahamian moon and Jan revealed some more of his past. It seems he was living in Norway when his wife passed away. He was 55 and restless, so he decided to move to America where his sister and her husband had been for some time. He got a job and worked for 20 years and got a nice little retirement at 75. He said he became bored with the retired life, was drinking too much and had gained a bit of weight, so after 3 years of this he decided to go sailing. He had been quite an avid sailor in his youth so knowledge of the sea was no obstacle.

This was when he decided to get a boat and try cruising for a while. He said that the broker who sold it to him committed a minor faux pas by saying are you buying this boat for your grandson? He said he did not say anything at the time, but to get some minor revenge he mails him a postcard about every year to let him know where he has been cruising and of all the beautiful young ladies he met (some exaggeration involved here but still for fun). Jan says cruising is a state of mind, not how old you are. There is just some basic equipment you must have, a good anchor windless, a couple of electric winches for handling the halyards and sheets. He says everything about his health has been fine except for a little trouble with arthritis and his teeth. In 10 years of cruising it has helped his health rather than cause any problems. He says he usually sails with friends from his sailing club or four nieces and nephews and their families. To occupy his spare time, when not doing that, he is learning to play the guitar ~ quite well, he gave us a sample ~ and learning to speak Spanish. This blew my mind. Two of my friends Bill and Carol just sold their boat. They are 59 and said they are just too old to be cruising. Well, I guess they will see when they read this article that they quit about 20 years too early. We smoked a couple of Cuban cigars and Jan went back to his boat.

When I got up to see the sunrise and had my usual lazy cup of coffee in the cockpit, Jan was pulling up his hook heading for Freeport. Grand Bahama. I had given him one of my books so he had my address, I yelled over as he was leaving, "Hey Jan, send me a card like you do that broker, when you can." He waved and sailed off over the horizon into his eighty-eighth year of cruising through life, and that just goes to prove it's never too late for the achievable dream.

My mate, Nora, for 25 years.

NIGHT CROSSING

Charter Capt. Song
Music by Jerr Francis, Dock Master in Bimini
Words by Frank Papy & Steve Ackin

Rolling down a long dark wave
With the wind ablowin'down the back o' me neck,
The old wheel is pullin' starboard she calls,
Lurin' this sleepy bastard into the reef and wreck.

I'd like to sheet out on the mizzen
but there's nobody else on deck.
They're all down in their snug warm bunks
With the blankets pulled over their heads
But I'll struggle through by the dawn be due
And stronger for it, so my old man said.

Headed west to my wife and child
As sure as my compass is true.
A two week charter is over again
And some good lovin' I know I'm due.
I look for lights but I know I am soon
though I'm pushing her pretty hard.

All I see burnt on my eyes are numbers
From the blood red compass card.
My salt caked brain fights dreams
Some of the future and past, in and out
Like the rolling tide

Nature's serving examples are seen.
Try to make fast to the moment you're in,
If you know what I mean.

Capt. Frank M. Papy

Author & Publisher
Cruising Guide to the Florida Keys
&
Contributing Editor
Yachtsman's Guide to the Bahamas

⊷ ⚓ ⊷

87425 Old Highway, #88
Islamorada, FL 33036
305-852-2326
www.cruising guide to the florida keys.com

Ordered by:

Name: _____

Address: _____

City: _____ State:_____ Zip:_____

Telephone Number: (_____) _____

Qty.	Title / Description		Price	Amount
	Cruising Guide To The Florida Keys	@	$19.95	$
	Yachtsman's Guide To The Bahamas	@	$39.95	
	Sailing... Impressions, Ideas, and Deeds	@	$12.95	
		Sub Total		
		Florida residents add 7.5% sales tax		
		Shipping and handling @ 2.50 per book		
	Total Books	Grand Total		$

Autograph To: _____

Mail To: _____

Name: _____
<small>(If different than ordered by)</small>

Address: _____

City: _____ State:_____ Zip:_____

Autograph To: _____

Mail To: _____

Name: _____
<small>(If different than ordered by)</small>

Address: _____

City: _____ State:_____ Zip:_____

Please make checks payable and mail to:
Frank M. Papy, 87425 Old Hwy, #88, Islamorada, FL 33036

~ 152 ~